GW00393650

A GAME DIVIDED

A
GAME DIVIDED

PETER McFARLINE

HUTCHINSON OF AUSTRALIA

HUTCHINSON GROUP (Australia) Pty Ltd
30–32 Cremorne Street, Richmond, Victoria, 3121

London Melbourne Sydney Auckland
Wellington Johannesburg
and agencies throughout the world

First published 1977
© Peter McFarline 1977
Set in Times by Modgraphic Pty Ltd, Adelaide
Printed and bound at Griffin Press Ltd, Adelaide

National Library of Australia
Cataloguing in Publication Data:

McFarline, Peter.
  A Game Divided.

ISBN 0 09 130681 7 Paperback.
ISBN 0 09 130680 9.

1. Cricket—England. I. Title.

796.35865

ONE

There was every reason to believe the 1977 Australian tour to England would be a successful and exciting one. That it turned out neither was due to a remarkable series of events which shattered the staid and well-ordered corridors of cricket like a nuclear explosion.

The euphoria created by the Centenary Test match in Melbourne in March quickly disappeared with the revelation in May that Sydney-based television tycoon and businessman Mr Kerry Packer had signed 35 of the world's top cricketers to take part in a series of matches in Australia in the summer of 1977–78. The formation of the Packer troupe, or circus as it was quickly dubbed, had been conducted in secret over a number of months. As details of the venture became known, it caused the greatest upheaval the game has known.

And while this was going on, the 1977 tourists surrendered the Ashes to England with scarcely a fight, drawing the Jubilee Test at Lord's then losing in rapid succession at Manchester, Trent Bridge and Leeds, before drawing a rain-affected Fifth Test at The Oval. Yet, on 17 March, when the touring party of 17 players was named only hours after Australia had gained an historic 45-run victory over England in the Centenary Test, the portents of Australia's decline had not become apparent.

Certainly, the team which had earned the title of champions of the world by a crushing Ashes win in the 1974–75 series against England, a successful tour there in 1975 and a stunning 5–1 decision over the West Indies at home in 1975–76, had had its moments of worry in the summer of 1976–77. The Pakistanis' short tour of Australia then had unearthed some old problems, particularly the one of handling class pace bowling which Imran Khan and Sarfraz Nawaz exploited with ferocity in the Third Test at Sydney, which saw the visitors triumph by eight wickets. Captain Greg Chappell, however, made sure that much hard work was done by his players on the short tour of New Zealand and the party returned, geared for the Centenary Test, having won the first and drawn the second of the two Tests played. That hard work earned its own reward on 17 March when the Australians captured the last six England wickets for 71 runs to snatch a memorable victory in the game that commemorated 100 years of Test cricket between the two countries.

Victory was tempered that morning when the chairman of the Australian selection panel, Mr Phil Ridings announced that Dennis Lillee, arguably the finest fast bowler in the world, would be unavailable for the four and a half month Jubilee tour. Lillee, it was said, had received medical advice that the stress fractures in his vertebrae were in danger of permanent damage if he undertook the tour. There was more to it than that, however. The selectors had had an idea since December that their trump card would not be available. The Western Australian had devoted more than a fair share of his sweat and skill to Australian cricket for the previous six years; now he wanted to spend more time with his family in Perth. As well, he had just signed on as a sporting commentator with the television show 'A Current Affair'. What the world didn't know then, was that there was a spectre looming large in the thoughts of Lillee and many of his friends . . . Kerry Francis Bullmore Packer. What was odd about Lillee's situation was that he had denied the story of his unavailability in his column in the Melbourne *Sun-News Pictorial* for two weeks after it had been broken in the Melbourne *Age*, and the *Australian*.

Whatever his reasoning for that, Lillee's loss to Greg Chappell's campaign was immense. The summer of 1976–77 had been probably the most successful in Lillee's distinguished career. In six Test matches that summer (three against Pakistan, two against New Zealand and one against England), he had taken 47 wickets at a cost of 21.64 runs each, battling his back injury, hamstring trouble and sore feet on wickets that generally favoured the batsmen. He had always been a willing worker on the unresponsive English wickets, though like most

2

Australian fast bowlers he nurtured a deep and undying resentment of their preparation.

No Lillee meant a place for an aspiring fast bowler in the touring party, although the selectors, Messrs Phil Ridings, Neil Harvey and Sam Loxton were now left in the position of having to gamble on the fitness of Lillee's fast partner, Jeff Thomson.

Thomson had suffered a severe shoulder injury on Christmas Eve in Adelaide, the first day of the First Test against Pakistan, when he collided with team-mate Alan Turner in attempting a caught and bowled chance off Zaheer Abbas. At first it was thought Thomson's right shoulder was so severely damaged that he would never bowl again, but an operation to insert a steel pin in the joint worked wonders. Thirteen days after the accident, on 5 January, Thomson's manager, Mr David Lord, informed Australian Cricket Board chairman Mr Bob Parish that his client would be fit for selection for the tour.

Australian touring teams to England traditionally include a surprise or two, but there were more than a couple when the 17 names rolled off the teleprinters just after 8 o'clock that night. The team was: Greg Chappell, Queensland, captain, 28 years, 47 Tests; Rod Marsh, Western Australia, vice-captain, 29 years, 48 Tests; Ray Bright, Victoria, 22 years, 0 Tests; Gary Cosier, South Australia, 23 years, 9 Tests; Ian Davis, New South Wales, 23 years, 12 Tests; Geoff Dymock, Queensland, 31 years, 4 Tests; David Hookes, South Australia, 21 years, 1 Test; Kim Hughes, Western Australia, 23 years, 0 Tests; Mick Malone, Western Australia, 26 years, 0 Tests; Rick McCosker, New South Wales, 30 years, 17 Tests; Kerry O'Keeffe, New South Wales, 27 years, 21 Tests; Len Pascoe, New South Wales, 26 years, 0 Tests; Richie Robinson, Victoria, 30 years, 0 Tests; Craig Serjeant, Western Australia, 25 years, 0 Tests; Jeff Thomson, Queensland, 26 years, 17 Tests; Max Walker, Victoria, 28 years, 29 Tests; Doug Walters, New South Wales, 31 years, 64 Tests.

Thomson and McCosker, who had had his jaw broken batting in the Centenary Test, were selected pending fitness tests, which they subsequently passed, although McCosker did not arrive in England until 14 May following an operation on his jaw in Sydney. The shocks included the omission of New South Wales all-rounder Gary Gilmour and left-handed

3

opening bat Alan Turner. Gilmour had played in Australia's six Tests over the summer, but had had a poor season. It transpired, after his abject bowling in the Centenary Test, that he had been carrying an achilles tendon injury for most of the summer, a fact he had kept secret from the selectors. For this oversight, he received harsh punishment. Turner, whose form had dropped away so much that he had been excluded from the Centenary Test side, could count himself unlucky also, especially as the selectors named only two opening batsmen— Ian Davis and McCosker—and only one of them was fully fit. That was to prove a costly mistake.

The absence of Lillee had paved the way for the fiery New South Welshman Len Pascoe to make the tour. Pascoe had been left out of his State side for the first two Sheffield Shield matches of the season because of the presence of West Indian Andy Roberts, but had made his mark in the remaining six games with 27 wickets at 23.00 runs each. The Queensland left-arm bowler Geoff Dymock was included at Gilmour's expense, an odd decision as Dymock, at 31, had failed to establish himself as a Test-class bowler in four attempts and was considered by most to be in the twilight of his career.

The most marked aspect of the touring squad was its inexperience. Ten of the 17 were making their first tour to England. Two of the young batsmen, the Western Australians Kim Hughes and Craig Serjeant, had yet to play a Test match, although they had had successful Shield seasons and Hughes had toured New Zealand. Another, David Hookes, had made his Australian debut in the Centenary Test, after scoring five centuries in six innings for his State, the first Australian to achieve the feat. Another, Gary Cosier, had played only nine Tests, and yet another, Ian Davis, 12. Throw in Victorian Richie Robinson, who hadn't won his Test match spurs, despite centuries in four successive matches in the domestic competition, and it meant six of the team's front-line batsmen had played 22 Tests between them. Two of the bowlers, Western Australian medium-pacer Mick Malone and Victorian left-arm spinner Ray Bright also had no Test match experience. The team was, quite rightly, labelled the most inexperienced to leave Australia's shores. It was soon to be called much worse than that!

4

TWO

The Australians arrived at Heathrow airport late on the morning of 22 April to be greeted by a sight that was to dog them for nearly a month: heavily overcast skies, persistent rain and cold winds.

The 29-hour flight from Sydney had provided some highlights, especially to two senior team members who successfully attacked the Qantas Sydney-to-London drinking record. Team manager Len Maddocks, who toured England as second wicket-keeper with the ill-fated 1956 team, had laid down his demands for discipline at a team meeting in Sydney the night before departure. These included the banning of players wearing advertising insignia on any of their cricket clothes, a demand that was acceded to by every one of the 17. Unfortunately, such a high standard of discipline and spirit was not seen again.

Two hours after touch-down, captain Greg Chappell and Maddocks were facing the combined England and Australian press at the party's London base hotel, the Waldorf. Rod Marsh and Doug Walters, still flushed with the success of their nerve-deadening flight, provided the comic relief as Chappell said what he was expected to say: 'It will be a good series—the teams are evenly matched. No, there will be no bouncer war. Yes, Jeff Thomson is fit. No, I haven't made up my mind if this will be my last overseas tour.' Maddocks made his point, rather light-heartedly, that he was 'here for a holiday' and was probably lucky that the Fleet Street representatives had been mellowed by several glasses of champagne beforehand. There was, of course, no mention of the drama that was to begin unfolding; not a whisper that one of the tourists—Jeff

Thomson—had been signed by the Packer troupe only hours before he boarded the jet at Sydney.

The Australians had scheduled four days of net practice at Lord's before their first match, against the Duchess of Norfolk's XI in the traditional tour opener at Arundel Castle in West Sussex. England in April is, well England in April, and as a result three of the practices were washed out. The first hadn't done much for the confidence of the younger batsmen either. On two damp, underprepared wickets at the famous Lord's nursery, Jeff Thomson in his first serious work-out since the Adelaide accident, and Len Pascoe made the ball jump and slide dangerously, leaving a succession of scorch marks on the bodies of Craig Serjeant and Ian Davis, who had suffered the misfortune of batting first. Such a pounding caused Gary Cosier to declare the only remedy was 'to slog', a method he employed to his detriment for the next two months.

Thomson's enthusiastic start had its repercussions. His speed at the nets had been close to his best, but the effort left him with strained muscles in the upper right arm, which kept him out of teams for Arundel and Surrey. With the weather also against him, Thomson could manage only three overs—against Kent—before he finally got some hard work in the Somerset match at Bath on 20 May, a month after arriving in England.

Inside the walls of the medieval Arundel Castle, ancestral home of the late Duke of Norfolk, Chappell took nine players wearing Australian colours for the first time, plus Richie Robinson, to tackle a team led by the then untarnished Tony Greig and containing 10 men with Test-match experience. Under the first sun of the tour, the youngsters got away to a confident start. Craig Serjeant, the 25-year-old Western Australian right-hander who squeezed into the touring party with an undefeated century for his State against the MCC in the lead-up to the Centenary Test, was the first to impress. While the élite of England's cricket spectators sipped Moet Chandon and tucked into smoked salmon, Serjeant, opening an innings for the first time in his short career, hammered 65, including 8 fours, to all parts of the ground and a straight six off Phil Edmonds. Chappell served notice of his intentions with

44 and Serjeant's Western Australian team-mate Kim Hughes made a stylish 28. In a light-hearted atmosphere, England's Test candidates Peter Willey, 50, and Derek Randall got close to Australia's total but were denied by the slow swing of Gary Cosier, whose 4/18 off 6.3 overs gave the visitors a 24-run victory.

That was 27 April. In some ways, it was the only high point of the tour. From then on rain, poor form, the Packer affair and all its ramifications combined to produce a gradual but insistent decline in control and camaraderie that was instrumental in producing the team's abysmal record.

The tourists' first first-class fixture was the three-day game against Surrey at The Oval. It was the prelude to a frustrating month. Rain on the two days preceding the game made practice impossible, and there was no play on the first day.

On the second—Monday, 2 May—veteran Surrey captain John Edrich won the toss and made the Australians labour in the slow outfield and unresponsive wicket, while he ground his way to 70—just short of his 100th first-class century, which he was to achieve later in the season—and Graham Roope stroked an impressive 107 not out. Only Max Walker impressed with the ball, taking 3/70 off 25 overs, but Len Pascoe, Geoff Dymock and Kerry O'Keeffe were astray in line and length in their first serious outing. Torrential rain on the third and final day made sure the Australians did not bat, and two-thirds of the first match had been lost.

The first of the many trips out of London was to the historical cathedral city of Canterbury for the Kent match. Here the Australians felt the full brunt of the inclement spring: more torrential rain, biting winds and ice-laden air which sent nine of the party to the nearest department store for an unprecedented run on long johns. Thomson was judged fit enough to make his tour debut, but only got the opportunity to bowl three overs and display some potent trouble in his run-up. Thirteen hours and five minutes, out of a possible 18, were lost in this game, yet Craig Serjeant, 50, and the elegant Kim Hughes, 80 in 202 minutes, were able to show their undoubted talent in Australia's first innings of 7/240 declared, spread over three interrupted days. Most of the spare time was spent in

7

energetic soccer matches which had the Kent crowd intrigued, if not by the players' skill, then certainly by their vigour.

The Canterbury ground, which slopes nine feet from one side to the other, certainly does not take kindly to poor weather. As the groundsman explained, straight-faced, before the match: 'With a slope like that, the water has a bad habit of running to middle and forming puddles'. It certainly did on this occasion and the match was finally abandoned on the third day, with Kent reaching only 2/33 in its first innings. Chris Cowdrey, 19-year-old eldest son of Colin, made his first-class debut in this game, but like everyone else suffered from the rain. He did, however, claim his first wicket when Doug Walters was caught at third slip.

While the team's coach made its way through the rain and sleet to the south coast resort town of Hove, the eight Australian journalists travelling with them were able to savour the culinary delights of the famous Monastery restaurant at Rye, one of the Cinque ports which by dint of silting has been left stranded, about three miles from the Dover Strait. Like the cricketers, the press party was then a jovial collection.

The fixture against Sussex at Hove on 7, 9, and 10 May was to assume rather more historic proportions than it has in previous tours. But first, it was another rain-ruined affair on the field, with only Serjeant again providing any reason for satisfaction. His 55 not out, out of Australia's total of 1/111, was his third successive half-century, yet he had been slotted into the opening spot as a stop-gap measure while the team awaited the late arrival of Rick McCosker, now stranded in Sydney by a strike of air traffic controllers. Ian Davis failed for the third time, clean-bowled attempting to force the aging, but still wily John Snow. Sussex also boasted in its attack Imran Khan, the Pakistani of whom the Australians had rather alarming memories and who was later to cause a controversy in English cricket circles as Sussex battled for a transfer for him from Worcestershire. Only 111 minutes of play was possible in this game and the impatience of Greg Chappell and his charges was starting to become obvious.

But such frustrations became secondary on Monday morning, 9 May. It was then, in Australia, that the Packer affair was unmasked for the first time.

8

THREE

The planning of the Packer troupe and the series of so-called Supertests in Australia during the summer of 1977–78 was undoubtedly the best kept secret in sporting history. From the time of its birth, in mid-1976, until May 1977 the general public, and indeed those not involved, including players and administrators, suspected nothing.

I first learnt about it, in general terms, in September 1976 and on 2 October, wrote an article in the *Age* outlining Channel 9's attempt to run a series of televised games, involving some of the world's best players. The story was quickly, and effectively, denied by Channel 9's Melbourne office. Attempts to learn more about the operation met a wall of silence for some months afterwards. Another Australian cricket writer, Alan Shiell, was also aware of the plan, but neither of us quite realized its extent, even by the time we came to break the story from Hove on 7 May, 1977, in time for the morning papers in Australia on 9 May. Shiell, a former South Australian Sheffield Shield batsman, who scored an unbeaten double century against the MCC tourists of 1965–66, and who has many close friends among the players, covered the England tour for the Rupert Murdoch group of newspapers, including the Adelaide *News*, Sydney *Daily Telegraph* and the *Australian*. We talked about the Packer plan many times during the summer and the early part of the England tour. We agreed to pool our resources and by 7 May had pieced together the broad outline. We also knew that two London papers, the *Daily Mail* and the *Sun*, were close to printing the story.

With play washed out after only an hour and 23 minutes,on Saturday at Hove, Shiell and I decided to approach Greg

Chappell for a comment about the Supertests. In a corridor outside the Australian dressing room, while the rest of the team watched the Rugby League Cup final on television, Chappell listened politely while we told him what we knew. Then, 'You can say this: "It sounds an interesting proposition—I'd like to know more about it".' And there was only a hint of a smile on his face. Chappell, had, in fact, signed his Packer contract two months earlier.

The stories, for the *Age* and the *Australian*, were filed that night from Hove in secret. Later, I returned to the home of former England fast bowler and Packer signatory John Snow and told him what I had written. With my permission, he then telephoned his friend and England captain Tony Greig to tell him the secret was out. Greig that night hosted a party at his magnificent home in Hove for both the Australian and English cricketers, and there was obviously more on his mind than partying. Early on the Sunday, the South African-born England captain took the extraordinary step of issuing a four-line statement through his agent, Reg Hayter, admitting that he had signed with Mr Packer. This had the effect of alerting every English newspaper to the story, which caused great chagrin to the *Daily Mail*'s outstanding sports columnist Ian Wooldridge. Late the previous week, Wooldridge had obtained more detail on the Packer plan than any other journalist. He had taken his information to his great friend, former Australian captain and well-known commentator and journalist Richie Benaud, and had it denied. But Wooldridge remained confident that he had a world exclusive, until the Greig statement and the feed-back from the Australian morning papers. Nevertheless, when the Fleet Street editions hit the pavements, it was the *Daily Mail* who had more detail than anyone else.

Benaud, who will act as tour principal during the Supertest series, had repeatedly denied any knowledge of the Packer deal prior to 5 April. It was then, he claims, that Packer approached his company, D. E. Benaud and Associates, to become consultants to the programme.

The sum total of the stories was that 35 of the world's top cricketers had been contracted to Mr Packer to play a series of six Supertests—planned then to be between Australia and the Rest of the World—and a series of one-day matches in Australia in the summer. The matches would be telecast exclusively by the Channel 9 network in Australia, of which Mr Packer is managing director. The players were being paid between $16,500 and $35,000 a year and most had contracts which extended over three summers. The contracts were binding and did not allow the players to play in other games which clashed with Packer fixtures.

The 35 players who had signed included 18 Australians, 13 of whom were touring England. The others were captain Ian Chappell, batsmen Ian Redpath and Ross Edwards, all of whom had retired from representative cricket, Dennis Lillee who had been unavailable for the tour because of medical and family reasons, and all-rounder Gary Gilmour, a surprise omission from the touring party. The 17 players who would make up the Rest of the World sides came from England (4), South Africa (5), Pakistan (4), and the West Indies (4).

The full-list was: AUSTRALIA: Ian Chappell, Greg Chappell, Rod Marsh, Doug Walters, Ray Bright, Ian Davis, David Hookes, Rick McCosker, Jeff Thomson, Len Pascoe, Kerry O'Keeffe, Richie Robinson, Max Walker, Mick Malone, Ian Redpath, Dennis Lillee, Ross Edwards and Gary Gilmour.
ENGLAND: Tony Greig, Derek Underwood, Alan Knott, John Snow.
SOUTH AFRICA: Barry Richards, Mike Procter, Graeme Pollock, Eddie Barlow, Denys Hobson.
PAKISTAN: Mushtaq Mohammad, Asif Iqbal, Majid Khan, Imran Khan.
WEST INDIES: Andy Roberts, Clive Lloyd, Vivien Richards, Michael Holding.

The only player at that time sought by Mr Packer who had not signed was the controversial Yorkshireman Geoff Boycott. As on many other aspects of the Packer story, there were two or more versions of what happened. On some points, I am convinced, not even the Packer organization is sure of what occurred. Boycott later claimed he had spoken to Mr Packer in Sydney early in 1977 about his project and had made a verbal agreement to sign. But when he was shown a copy of his

11

contract in England later, he found several points differing from his talk in Sydney and finally did not sign because he could foresee a clash between the television games and those for his beloved Yorkshire. But the *Bulletin*, the weekly news magazine owned in Sydney by Australian Consolidated Press, of which Mr Packer is chairman of directors, claimed negotiations had broken down because Boycott had insisted on appointing the captain of the Rest of the World squad.

Two weeks earlier, on 24 April, the South African newspaper, *Sunday Times*, had given a hint of the impending drama when it broke the news that four South African cricketers, Barry Richards, Eddie Barlow, Mike Procter and Graeme Pollock had 'signed lucrative contracts to play an eight-week series of matches throughout the world'. That little bombshell had been dropped by another South African, Lee Irvine, in a speech at which he announced his retirement from the first-class game in Johannesburg. The South African *Sunday Times* story got no publicity in England, mainly because Reuters news agency could not confirm it.

FOUR

The reaction around the world to the news of the Packer involvement in cricket was mainly disbelief, then shock and horror. The royal and ancient game, which had only so recently celebrated its centenary, was being assailed in a way never envisaged by the old guard authority that had ruled it so unequivocally and so conservatively. Wooldridge, in his *Daily Mail* story, had christened the 35 rebels the 'Dogs of Cricket' and it was a name the majority of cricket lovers thought appropriate.

But Wooldridge, in fact, came out in limited support for the move, at least in theory, '. . . far from being a shock development, I suggest that the only surprise about what happened at the weekend was that it was so long delayed. If the game's administrators failed to see it coming, then they are low in perception.'

The truth was that the game's administrators, in Australia, England and the other major cricket countries, had indeed failed to see it coming. There were cries of indignation that the players, and the Packer organization, had acted in an underhand and deceitful manner in their signing of the contracts. England's chairman of selectors Alec Bedser pointed out that, '. . . this could disrupt the whole structure of Test cricket . . . there is no fair comparison between cricket, a team game and such sports as golf and tennis'.

Len Maddocks, the Australian team manager, with 13 of the rebels in his team, made public his first reaction at Hove: 'I do not envisage the present development having a detrimental effect on this tour. But if any of them [the tourists] play for a side contrary to the jurisdiction of the Australian Board, they place their careers in jeopardy'. In Sydney on his return from the tour on 5 September, Maddocks was to admit that the Packer issue had had a disastrous effect on his team's morale. 'There were overtones of the Packer thing all the time. Everywhere we went, the media were on the subject.'

Jeff Stollmeyer, president of the West Indies Board of Control, was rather more conciliatory: 'I don't see how anyone can condemn the players. After all, their careers are not all that permanent. I do not think in the longer term that exhibition matches will attract either the interest or the gates that Test matches will'. Two and a half months later, Stollmeyer was voting, along with all other International Cricket Conference delegates, to ban the Packer players from Test cricket if they did not change their minds before 1 October.

On the morning of 9 May, Maddocks gathered his Australian team in their dressing room at Hove and told them that they were not allowed to talk to anyone about their dealings or their intentions regarding the troupe. According to all who were present, it was a pleasant enough meeting. Mr Maddocks had had his early morning disturbed by a series of telephone calls from Australian Cricket Board chairman Mr Bob Parish and secretary Alan Barnes. There was no suggestion, he was told, that any part or the whole of the team would be recalled to Australia. There was a tour of England on, and this was the players' prime concern.

As yet, few could see the ever-widening ripples. A boulder had been cast into cricket's basically smooth pond. The players, however, were more than happy to talk privately now that the secret was out. The large burden of silence had been lifted from their shoulders. At first, the more senior members of the team—Rod Marsh, Doug Walters, Richie Robinson, Max Walker, Kerry O'Keeffe—were enthusiastic, even expansive. They agreed that in all probability they faced a ban from Test, first-class, even club cricket. But the rewards were far greater in three years with the troupe, than any they could see coming from representing Australia for five years. Robinson, for instance, was nearing 30, yet had never played a Test for Australia, despite four centuries in four games in the 1976–77 domestic season. As basically a Sheffield Shield cricketer,

14

drawing $80 a game plus paltry expenses and some subsidiary revenue from sponsorship, his talent was not going to earn him a better standard of living. The Packer troupe, he explained, had given him that chance and he had no regrets about signing.

Walker, Marsh and Walters had long been advocates of better pay for top cricketers and as they were facing up to their last few years in the top strata of the game, along with Greg Chappell, Lillee and the England players John Snow and Greig, their reaction to the Packer plan was logical.

In the lounge of their Hove hotel, which the Australians had named, not facetiously, the 'Deadly' Dudley, the younger players, Ray Bright, 22, Ian Davis, 23, David Hookes, who turned 22 on 3 May, Mick Malone, 26, and Len Pascoe, 27, talked of their reasoning. The home they wanted to buy, the education they wanted for their children, the luxury items they couldn't reasonably see themselves affording while they attempted to make their names at the top of the cricket tree. Before the tour was over, at least four of them, Davis, Hookes, Malone and Pascoe, were to spend many hours worrying over the wisdom of their choice.

The four players left out of the squad seemed, then, unaffected. Only Gary Cosier, with two Test centuries and an average of 40.15 from only nine Test matches, could feel slighted. But he knew why: Packer's Australian team had been selected largely by former Test captain Ian Chappell, and Chappell had long been a public critic of Cosier's attitude to the game. Both Western Australian batsmen Craig Serjeant and Kim Hughes had yet to play a Test match. In fact, between them, they could lay claim to only three first-class seasons and Geoff Dymock, at 31 the oldest man in the team, could hardly have been looking forward to much longer in the first-class arena. Later in the tour, however, there were suggestions both within and without the team that the selectors were deliberately keeping the non-Packer men out of the Tests. Cosier and Dymock did not play in any one of the five encounters with Brearley's men; Hughes came into the side for the first time in the Fifth Test at The Oval and Serjeant, after a sturdy debut 81 at Lord's was surprisingly left out of the Third and Fourth Tests.

At no stage do I believe Chappell, Marsh and Walters let their choice of players be influenced by the drama going on around them. What appeared to happen was that the three selectors decided on a policy of playing their most experienced side in the Test matches, even though on most occasions some of the more experienced players had little or no form. By the time they realized this policy was incorrect, the series was lost and some reputations were in tatters. Mick Malone's success at The Oval immediately raised the question, 'what would have happened if . . .'?

But on 9 May, the over-riding impression from the Australians was one of sitting back and waiting for the Packer storm to break. They didn't have to wait long.

From the beginning, I was intensely critical of Mr Packer's plan to take over international cricket. I was convinced that his main interest was to make money from the venture, money that would flow on to the shareholders of his television company, TCN 9, Sydney. Along the way, he had offered a series of lucrative contracts to the world's best cricketers but then he had never been credited with being less than a tough, shrewd businessman. He had been alert enough to sense the discontent with which cricketers reviewed their lot. After all, the Australians in particular had been bringing in huge box office receipts for five years at least and their compensation, although improving slowly, had not improved enough. That, of course, was the fault of Australia's cricket administrators—both at Australian Cricket Board and State association level.

The long-term welfare of the game seemed, and still seems, to have little influence in Mr Packer's thinking. What he wanted all along—and he made no secret of it—was exclusive rights to cricket telecasts in Australia. Previous experience of the cricket World Cup, televised live to Australia in 1975, and the unqualified success of the Centenary Test, had pointed to such rights as a financial bonanza. If he got those, Mr Packer was prepared to let his Supertests fall into established cricket's hands. He had admitted as much privately and made it public after the failure of his discussions with the International Cricket Conference in London on 23 June.

During that meeting, Mr Packer had agreed to compromise

with the ICC on five significant points. Then he demanded the exclusive television rights in Australia when the existing agreement with the Australian Broadcasting Commission expired early in 1979. This the ICC quite rightly refused to agree to, and the talks finished. Outside the Lord's committee room, Mr Packer gave vent to his feelings to reporters: 'I am only in the arena because of my disagreement with the Australian Cricket Board. Had I got those TV rights, I was prepared to withdraw from the scene and leave the running of cricket to the Board. I will now take no steps to help anyone, every man for himself and the devil take the hindmost. I compromised so much that I felt strange in myself. I thought we were going to reach a period of breakthrough but the talks failed because of the stubbornness of the ICC. I have never wanted to control cricket, but I wanted and I would have expected to get exclusive rights when the current TV contracts ran out. I said I would go back under the control of the Australian Board, have shorter tours and withdraw from the scene completely if our network could have these rights and the players were not victimized.'

Even such a staunch Packer supporter as Rod Marsh was amazed by these remarks. Marsh, like the other senior players, had been lauding Mr Packer as the saviour of cricket. Now it appeared Mr Packer's interest in the game was not what it was thought by some to be.

Another of my objections was that, if the troupe became successful, it would have to be extended. The only way this could happen would be by skimming off the cream of the world's promising young cricketers, who had grown promising in the pastures nurtured by each of the ICC member countries. There was—and has been—no suggestion that the Packer organization will provide cricket competition at junior, school, club and even interstate levels to breed its own champions of the future. It is all very well, to argue, as Ian Chappell and Tony Greig have, that each Packer contract provides for every player to indulge in at least five coaching clinics per season. Such clinics are an excellent idea for fostering young boys' interest in cricket. But who provides the competitions for these boys to use their new skills and enthusiasm? And who provides the

17

working hours—most of them honorary—to keep cricket going at the lower levels? The devotees, young and old, who form that now hackneyed phrase, 'established cricket'. Yet the players rising through the ranks would be lured as soon as the Packer troupe thought them eligible.

All this would occur if the troupe was successful, and if there had been no compromise between the troupe and the cricket establishment. At the time of writing, such compromise seems at least 18 months or two years away—if at all.

And what of the troupe, if it was not successful? The instability of the Australian television industry is well known in the broadcasting world. The fickleness of the viewing public has caused many a large advertiser to bemoan his investment. Given such a background, Mr Packer's gamble was enormous. That is his business, but gambling with the futures of the world's best cricketers is something more far reaching. Frankly, I cannot see the Australian public sustaining enough interest in an artificial series of cricket matches, played on makeshift wickets prepared in concrete vats and then transported into football and trotting venues, to keep the major sponsors that Mr Packer needs, interested for long enough to make the venture the success he hopes.

Cricket officials confirm that the two poorest-attended series in recent years have been the Rest of the World tour of England in 1970 and the Rest of the World in Australia in 1971–72. The troupe's initial games this summer could well give Mr Packer a promising start—from curiosity value—but the lure of Test matches between national representative teams cannot be replaced by a limitless bank account.

The comparison, made by many Packer supporters, between the growth of professionalism in tennis and golf, hardly bears weight. Both are individual sports for which the public was willing to pay large amounts of money to watch head-to-head contests between the best in the world. When shrewd men like Jack Kramer realized there was a fortune waiting to be made by the champions of tennis, they led them in a break-away movement from the 'shamateur' game, until finally the professionals won their point of recognition as the best in the business playing for the highest rewards. The position is not the same in cricket, where only in Australia and England at Test level, are there high financial returns. These high returns are quickly watered down by the necessity to spread the money around at every level to keep the game going. The Sheffield Shield competition for instance, is not even now in a position of being a profit-making concern. Neither is the county championship in England where, in fact, a majority of the 17 counties face a continuous battle to stay solvent. In cricket, there is more to professionalism than keeping the top-class players well paid and happy.

Lastly, the contracting of the players for the Packer troupe was carried out behind a wall of secrecy and silence. The secrecy is understandable, for, as Packer himself explained, 'in business, you never tell your competitor what you are planning'. But right up to the start of the tour of England, many of the players involved could have been seen as seeking the best of both worlds. Four of the Australians, Greg Chappell, Doug Walters, Richie Robinson and Rod Marsh were captains of their respective Sheffield Shield sides. As such, they met with ACB officials Bob Parish, Ray Steele and Tim Caldwell several times during the 1976–77 season as part of the Cricket Committee formed to give Australian players their first chance to express their wants and needs to the ACB. And at one of those meetings at least, the four captains, while pressing for more money and better conditions, knew about the Packer deal.

As late as March, Greg Chappell was deciding between offers to return to Adelaide to play for South Australia or to stay in Queensland to continue with his adopted State for five more years. Robinson, too, was making moves to transfer to the Melbourne club Essendon for a good coaching fee. To say those players were not aware of the impending bans on them by the ICC and domestic authorities is not true. Most of the Australians openly admitted in May that they were well aware they could be banned from cricket at all levels, despite the assurances they had been given by the Packer organization before signing the contracts that their normal cricket would not be affected.

The secrecy extended so far that a number of the players for

19

whom Packer was bidding were not even allowed to take their contracts to lawyers for perusal before signature. In some cases, players had not even had time to read through the eight pages of foolscap that made up the first contracts. The contracts also made no secret of the fact that the promoter (J. P. Sport Pty Ltd) expected a head-on clash with the major cricket authorities. In clause 3(b)(1) of the contract, it was stipulated that the player will not: '. . . play in any cricket match other than a match of a tour without the consent in writing of the promoter, first had and obtained . . .' And the *Bulletin*, when it released full details of the plan in its edition of 14 May, made no secret of the fact that the contracted players would be available for Test, Shield and club games only when they did not clash with Packer games. The magazine also pointed out that the Packer matches between Australia and the Rest of the World would coincide with the dates of the Test matches against India.

Australian Cricket Board officials felt most strongly that the players had not been completely honest with them and it was this feeling that had much to do with the hard-line policy that the ACB adopted initially.

There was, however, one major benefit from the whole affair. Whatever the outcome, it had underlined the sad state, generally, of cricketers' incomes. Authorities around the world now realized what they should have realized years before: that the discontent of the players was so widespread, the opportunity for an entrepreneur to lure players into a commercial venture was too good to be missed. Now, at last, the controlling bodies would have to pay their bread-winners something like their full due. The proof of this came even before the 1977 series was over. For the last two Test matches, a group of English businessmen paid over £9000 (A$14,400) a Test to the England side. Then the giant insurance company, Cornhill, announced a £1 million (A$1.6 million) sponsorship agreement with the Test and County Cricket Board over five years. Most importantly, it guaranteed that every player representing England would get at least £1000 (A$1600) a Test match.

John Cornell, one of the men responsible for the original

troupe concept, and a principal of the company, J. P. Sport Pty Ltd which was formed to be the promoter of the Supertest series, claimed it was the players' desire for better rewards from the game that enabled the scheme to be carried out in such secrecy. 'It was an indication of how keen the players were to make sure nothing became snarled up.'

It was obvious, too, that many more sponsors would come forward to answer the challenge to the authorized version of the game. The great pity was that this money had not been sought with enough vigour, or made available with such enthusiasm, before the advent of Mr Packer.

FIVE

While the forces for and against the Packer troupe massed for the inevitable confrontation, the Australians travelled on to Southampton for the game against Hampshire—and more rain-induced disappointment. This time not a ball was bowled as England's wettest spring for 100 years reached its climax. So desperate was Greg Chappell for some cricket for his charges that he even offered to bat in abysmal conditions—an offer that was politely rejected by the Hampshire captain Richard Gilliat. There was succour for some in the sponsor's tent and the lunch-time eloquence of the county's favourite son, John Arlott, but little to appease the tourists whose alternative sport, soccer, was getting more violent by the day. The wash-out was also a bitter disappointment to South African Barry Richards, for whom the match was part of a well-earned benefit. Already, three of his benefit games had suffered similar fates. The rain, he confided, had cost him well over £1000 (A$1600).

The excursion to Swansea, for the match against Glamorgan, was highlighted by the news that Tony Greig had lost the captaincy of England over his involvement in the Packer troupe. The United Kingdom Cricket Council, the game's supreme body in Britain, in an emergency meeting on Friday, 14 May, ruled that the South African-born all-rounder was not to be considered as captain for the forthcoming series against Australia. 'His action', read the Council's statement in part, 'has inevitably impaired the trust which existed between the cricket authorities and the captain of the England side'. F. R. Brown, chairman of the Council and a former England leader, added, 'The captaincy of the England team involves close liaison with the selectors in the management, selection and development of England players for the future and clearly Tony Greig is unlikely to be able to do this as his stated intention is to be contracted elsewhere during the next three winters'.

So the Establishment had struck the first blow, not altogether unexpectedly. Greig's demise had been freely forecast since the news of his involvement broke at the start of the week. And it became something of a certainty, when, two days before the Council met, he held a press conference at the Sussex County Ground at Hove, where he admitted, without provocation, that he had acted for Mr Packer in the recruiting and signing of many of the overseas players now involved in the troupe. Signing with the enemy was bad enough. Acting on his behalf was tantamount to being a cricketing Judas, in official eyes anyway, and Greig, who had helped England's cricket back onto its feet in the 14 Tests he had commanded, was summarily evicted. He was to be left in no doubt as to the cricketing public's feelings towards him in the months to come either . . . his ears were soon to be accustomed to the discordant boos and jeers, even from his once-adoring fans in Sussex.

At that same meeting on 14 May, the Council decided to make no decision about the eligibility of the four England rebels, Greig, Underwood, Knott and Snow for the Tests against Australia. They had wielded the axe on Greig's captaincy—the next step, the Council felt, belonged to the Test and County Cricket Board.

Immediately, conjecture began as to Greig's successor. The logical favourite was his vice-captain on the Indian and Australian tour, Mike Brearley. Brearley was certainly bred for the job. He had led Middlesex to the county championship in 1976 and had an outstanding scholastic record at City of London school and Cambridge University. Against him were his inexperience—only 8 Tests—and his inability to lay claim to a permanent opening batsman's place in the England side. Inevitably, the cry for the recall of self-rejected Geoff Boycott became louder, although how such a move could be justified in the light of the Yorkshireman's dedication to his own ends was beyond my comprehension.

23

Greig, nonetheless, went down unrepentant. His comment on his dismissal was: 'Obviously, I am disappointed that my reign as England captain has come to an end just as we were beginning to put things together. From a personal point of view, the only redeeming factor is that I have sacrificed cricket's most coveted job for a cause which I believe could be in the best interests of cricket the world over'. Later that night, he admitted he had given much thought to telling Lord's about the Packer scheme after signing the contract. 'But you mustn't forget the show was on the road by then.'

The wrath of Fleet Street had been trained on Greig for several days, a remarkable reversal by a group of men who, less than two months before, had stood to give him a standing ovation after his final Centenary Test press conference. Now, with his sacking, some softer words were spoken, especially by another former England captain Colin Cowdrey who eloquently portrayed his distraction in the *Sunday Telegraph*: 'I was confident that England would win back the Ashes under Tony Greig's leadership. Alas, a sickening temptation has been put his way and in the moment of euphoria after his triumphant march through India and the excitement of the Centenary Test, he succumbed'.

John Woodcock, the respected cricket correspondent for *The Times*, was somewhat harsher. In a front page article on Greig, Woodcock came up with the extraordinary statement, '. . . after all, he is not British through and through . . .'

But the ruckus over Greig was not the Australians' main worry as they arrived in Swansea to be greeted by leaden skies and the news that it had been raining in Wales for a week. And when the first day's play against Glamorgan was abandoned, the tourists could lay claim to their first record of the tour. Of the scheduled 88 hours of cricket in their first five games, they had managed to be on the field for only 22 hours and 56 minutes. And that, said the experts, was the wettest start to any Australian tour.

The appalling weather gave rise once again to the old argument that tours to England should start later—in mid-May—to avoid the generally wet April weather. 'I have been here four times', said Greg Chappell, 'and every April has been the same'. It is an argument I believe will be accepted, especially as Australians will probably never again be asked to undergo the arduous five month long traditional tour. The time for shorter tours has arrived.

The game began on time on the second day, as the sun shone, and the Australian pace bowlers Pascoe, Walker and Dymock ran through the county side, dismissing it for 172. But Davis failed again, with 14, as did Hughes, 4, and Robinson, tried as an opener for the first time, 20. Hard-hitting by Cosier, 56, and Walters, 36, enabled Walters, leading Australia for the first time in the absence of Chappell and Marsh, to declare 19 runs behind, on the third morning. Glamorgan, untroubled by a lack-lustre attack, hustled to a second innings declaration of 4/164, leaving the visitors 184 to get in 40 minutes and 20 overs. After medium-pacer Malcolm Nash had sent the first five batsmen back at a personal cost of 24 runs, the score was a pathetic 6/39. Only resolute defence by spinners O'Keeffe, 21 not out, and Bright, 26 not out, earned a less than honourable draw.

With the one-day internationals only two weeks away, and the First Test less than a month, the Australians had major problems. The weather had been desperately unkind and the rigorous structure of the tour itinerary prevented long hours at the practice nets, which most of the young batsmen craved. As well, there seemed to be little interest in the tour; the Packer saga was raging with almost each day bringing a new development and the story of the tourists' progress relegated generally to a few paragraphs well buried.

On 15 May, the South African Cricket Association announced it would follow whatever line the International Cricket Conference took on the outlaws, even if that meant banning the five South African players involved. It seemed South Africa, no longer an ICC member, was using the controversy to shore up its claims for re-entry to membership.

And Tony Greig's statement of the previous week, that the Packer troupe would be of benefit to every rank and file cricketer in the country, was also causing a furore.

'As yet', said Jack Bannister, secretary of the Players' Association, 'I have neither seen, heard nor read anything which convinces me that the proposed deal can have any beneficial effect on players' financial conditions in this country'. The Association represents all but one of the first-class cricketers playing in England and was in the unique position of sporting as members both Packer and non-Packer players. Snow, who had aligned himself with the rebels, was a member of the Association executive.

The Packer affair had so far not really touched the tourists; the brunt of public and official ire had been directed at Greig, and his England team-mates Knott and Underwood. The tourists, 13,000 miles away from home, could only gauge Australian reaction from friends and family. Officially, at least, the Australian reaction was to wait until the tour concluded in September before taking action, although this was to change in the intervening months. The West Country games, and the interlude in Wales, seemed to have removed the team from the mainstream of controversy.

The ancient walled city of Bath, with its Roman baths and superb architecture, is a pleasing prospect at any time. When brilliant summer weather appeared for the first time on the tour, the Australians were entitled to tackle their match against a strong Somerset side with gusto; that they were beaten by seven wickets underlined a nagging fear held by some that too many of the side lacked the mental power to address themselves to the problems caused by playing cricket in conditions foreign to them. With 10 newcomers to England in the group, there was obviously a need for some leadership from the experienced players; at times, it was missing, and so was the camaraderie that typified teams led by Ian Chappell and Richie Benaud.

Nevertheless, there was great interest in the Somerset game. McCosker, first held in Sydney by his doctors, then delayed for a week because of a strike of air traffic controllers, was to make his 1977 debut. So too was a giant of a man they called the Big Bird; West Indian Joel Garner, whose height, 6 ft $7\frac{1}{2}$ ins, had given his fast bowling a special quality in his Test debut series against Pakistan. Now Somerset had secured his services from the Lancashire League for week-day games only and he got away to an auspicious start, having McCosker caught at second slip for two in the first over of the match. Serjeant failed for the first time, then the large crowd settled down to a morning of vintage Chappell, who at one stage hit Garner for 3 fours and a six off four deliveries.

With Cosier applying himself for the first time on tour, Chappell raced to 99 at lunch, only missing his century in a session by dint of losing the strike. Such a feat, however, did not impress the irrepressible Walters who delivered his captain a trenchant blast at the interval. 'You just won't accept a challenge', smirked Walters whose penchant for a century between breaks is well known. Garner had his revenge soon after, yorking Chappell for 113—his 50th first-class century— Cosier for 44, and Marsh for 3. Hookes, who failed in Swansea, retained his poor run, bowled by a good inswinger from young all-rounder Ian Botham, whose form had convinced the Somerset lads of his future as an England player. Indeed, that day, Botham learned of his selection in the MCC side to play Australia at Lord's in the traditional Test warm-up game nine days later.

The Australians collapsed after lunch, slumping from 2/177 to 232 all out with veteran medium-pacer Graham Burgess taking 5/25 off 9.3 overs—and in his benefit year too. Worse was to follow for the tourists: Thomson, in his first serious workout of the tour, was no-balled 12 times in his first four overs by Dicky Bird as Somerset openers Brian Rose and Peter Denning handled the attack with ease in a stand of 81.

Next day, Somerset coasted to 5/340 declared, with Rose going onto 110 not out, and young batsmen Ian Botham, 59, and Phil Slocombe, 55 not out, hitting hard. When Australia batted, McCosker was run out for 2, and Botham claimed Cosier for 2, before Serjeant, 50, and Hookes became associated in a century stand. Hookes, showing his wares for the first time, raced to 85 not out off 66 deliveries by stumps and completed his century in 80 deliveries on the last morning. But Somerset was left only 181 to win, a victory it achieved via a powerful 53 from Viv. Richards and another contribution from Botham, 39 not out.

Chappell was unperturbed by the result; Thomson, short of match practice, short of bowling rhythm, was his main worry now. The explosive fast bowler had a fitness query over him, which only he could answer, although Chappell suspected he was saving his best for the Tests. Nevertheless, with the side still not manifesting its home-grown talents, an in-form Thomson would have been a morale booster.

The bleak weather returned for the game against Gloucestershire at Bristol, where at least victory helped the tourists' outlook on life. While some fortunate players and journalists basked in the sun with 100,000 others as Manchester United upset Liverpool in the FA Cup final at Wembley, Chappell decided to bat on a treacherous piece of ground that went under the name of the wicket at the ugly Bristol arena, whose old railway carriage of a press-box forever shuddered dangerously in the constant wind. By the time veteran Brian Brain had finished with 7/51 off 19 overs, Australia was out for 154. Only Victorian spinner Ray Bright, 53 not out, could handle the unpredictable bounce which bit at the ankles or thrust at the head every other delivery. Days like this are made for Max Walker, who took 7/19 off 11.3 overs as he and Mick Malone, 3/44 off 11 overs, shot the county out for 63. Australia, batting again on the first day, lost McCosker once more for 2, then watched in admiration on the second day as Chappell gave a masterly display of batting in atrocious conditions to hit 102.

Gloucestershire, set 342, never looked likely with Pascoe, 4/36, turning in his best performance and Bright claiming another four. Pascoe previously had tried to live up to his pre-tour publicity for fire, pitching too short on the placid English wickets and receiving much professional punishment. But, despite his total inability to come to terms with time, or the team bus, he had been working hard on his problems. And it was here that he first sowed the seed in Chappell's mind that he could be a useful addition to the Test team, pitching up and allowing the seam and the turf to do the work.

With a day in hand, manager Len Maddocks agreed to Gloucestershire's request for a limited-over practice match, a decision which angered many of the players, especially as the manager had refused a Glamorgan request to play an extra day in lieu of the one lost to rain. In any event, the match served no useful purpose, although Hughes and Walters both slammed half-centuries as the tourists coasted home.

The tour selectors, still perplexed by the inconsistency of form of most of the team, gave the fringe players Serjeant, Cosier, Hughes, Hookes and Dymock their chance against a young MCC side at Lord's.

The cricket Establishment had readied itself for the fight against Packer by the time the tourists arrived at Lord's for the start of the MCC game, on 25 May. The choice of Mike Brearley to lead the MCC was a clear indication of their plans to appoint a successor to Tony Greig, and it was no surprise when Brearley, 35, was named as England captain for the three one-day Prudential Trophy matches on 2, 4, and 6 June. The Middlesex scholar knew he had only to lead and perform moderately well to gain the Test captaincy. The England selectors, Alec Bedser, John Murray, Ken Barrington and Charlie Elliott had left the Packer trio Greig, Underwood and Knott out of the MCC side, a hint most of us mistakenly construed to mean the end of the Test road for these veterans. More importantly, the International Cricket Conference had called an emergency meeting at Lord's on 14 June 'to discuss the situation resulting from a declared intention to stage an unofficial series' during 1977–78.

The next day, 26 May, the Test and County Cricket Board announced that it had informed its selection committee to pick the England teams for the Prudential Trophy and the first three Test matches strictly on merit. In other words, Greig, Underwood and Knott had been spared any punishment at least until the full ICC meeting scheduled for 26 and 27 July, a meeting which was expected to act on the recommendations of the emergency meeting.

While the politics were being thrashed out in the stern committee rooms overlooking the headquarters of cricket, the Australian batsmen were once again lowering their side into trouble. After Chappell won the toss, they failed against the swing of Mike Hendrick, the Derbyshire fast bowler now fully fit after several years of injury which had made his Test appearances intermittent. Serjeant was his first victim and Hendrick followed by claiming Cosier for 19 and Hookes for 3. Only Hughes, with a stylish 60 in two and a half hours mastered the attack and Hendrick finished with 4/28 in a total of 194.

The bowlers reprieved their team-mates, scuttling MCC for 136 after Serjeant began the debacle, throwing down Brearley's stumps from side-on in the third over of the innings. Only Derek Randall with an attractive half-century showed any class as Thomson (still no-balling, but bowling with increased venom) Walker, Dymock and O'Keeffe shared the wickets. Even so, Randall was missed twice in his innings, a flaw in the team make-up that was to grow into a gaping wound before the series was very old.

Australian tourists in recent trips to England have developed the habit of not attempting the sharp chances in minor games, which are often played in cold weather. The 1977 variety was no different, yet when the Test matches came, their catching standard was the worst of any Australian side in memory. McCosker at last showed form when the Australians batted again, struggling in the early part of his four-hour stay but eventually finishing with 73. Chappell, too, was in form with 44 but the others, notably Cosier, Hookes and Hughes, all failed and MCC was left 294 to win on the last afternoon. Brearley, Randall and Barlow made useful contributions, but the speed of Thomson, 3/50, and the inviting spin of O'Keeffe proved too much. Australia gained its second tour victory by 79 runs and on face value had reason to feel pleased. In reality, the pace bowlers were the only division of the party paying their way. Chappell's form was faultless, but in Australian teams of recent years, few of the other batsmen would have been considered.

The Worcestershire match, the last before the one-day series, was drawn but the batsmen showed some improved form. Thomson, whose form at Lord's had been encouraging, was a late withdrawal with a recurrence of muscle strain in his upper right arm, and a delighted section of the press immediately said he would not see out the tour. The enigmatic Thomson, however, was doing more than his fair share of foxing. Davis, 83, and McCosker, 33, managed the team's first half-century stand, Davis bringing himself out of the batting horrors with a five hour occupation of the crease. Then Chappell hit his third century in four matches, a merry affair that took just over two hours and ended in a flurry of boundaries as he battled against a foot injury, which forced him from the crease at 100.

With a little help from Walters and Robinson, the total of 358 was the highest of the tour so far. Slipshod Australian fielding let Worcestershire's openers Glen Turner and Alan Ormrod in for a century opening, but the innings folded in the face of Pascoe's 4/40 and intelligent left-arm spin from Bright, 5/91. Pascoe and Malone, on trial for a Test berth in this game, bowled long spells from the same end, with Pascoe finishing well ahead. Although Davis, Cosier and Robinson hustled runs in the second innings, the game petered out to a no-result.

One-day cricket has proved a lifesaver to England in recent years. There are three one-day competitions held each season, and attendances at all three are much greater than at county fixtures. So the now established Prudential Trophy series of games against each touring side excites plenty of interest in the host country at least. The selectors went for their strongest squad of 14 including, as instructed, the Packer rebels Greig, Knott and Underwood, and young players Ian Botham (Somerset), Geoff Miller (Derbyshire), Graham Barlow (Middlesex) and Peter Willey (Northamptonshire).

The Australians, on the other hand, displayed their characteristic lack of seriousness for the limited (55 overs each) encounter, shelving their selection problems by saying every member of the seventeen-man squad would play in at least one of the three £2000 ($3200) winner-take-all encounters. The biggest problem was still Thomson's arm injury. He bowled energetically at the Old Trafford nets the day before the first one-day international, and in the bar that night, induced me to join him in a bet that he would be in the side for the morning. Chappell quickly sealed the fate of that money, when he announced that Thomson wouldn't be risked and that Walker, Malone and Pascoe would all play. 'Thommo's injury is not serious; we just want him 100 per cent for the Test matches', explained the captain, adding that the Tests were the only games he viewed as important.

Despite the build up to the series, it was pushed off the back page of the tabloids next morning. The new kid—Kerry Packer—was in town and had been making bold utterances on the Independent Television Network. It wasn't a pirate series at all, Mr Packer insisted, it was a Supertest series. 'I've sent telegrams to all the cricketing bodies, but they won't reply. I'm willing to compromise, but time is running out.' And, he added, cricket was the easiest sport in the world to take-over. 'Nobody bothered to pay the players what they were worth.'

In brilliant sunshine, before a packed Manchester crowd, the Prudential Trophy series began as the rest of the tour was to for Australia—disastrously. Chappell batted first on a patchy-looking strip and after four overs, Australia was 2/2. Davis was out in the second over, edging Lever into the slips and McCosker followed, cutting wildly at Willis to edge a catch to Knott. Chappell, 30, and Serjeant, 46, indulged in a brief stand and with no help from Walters or Hookes, Australia slumped to 6/94. Only the swashbuckling Marsh, 42 in 31 deliveries and the stubborn O'Keeffe, 16 not out, guided the score to a contestable 9/169 in the allotted time. England always looked the winner, but somehow found itself struggling after lackadaisical cricket had resulted in the running out of Barlow, 42, and Greig, 22. Barlow had been meandering back to the bowlers' crease after deciding against a second run when the eagle-eyed Marsh threw down his wicket, and Greig, prancing around after being struck on the thigh, was foiled by an alert Pascoe, following through. In the end, Knott and Old steered England home by two wickets, with Marsh claiming the £200 ($320) Man of the Match award.

Under overcast skies at Birmingham two days later, Chappell sent England in to bat. The big news was that Thomson was playing. He was not in the selected side, and as late as two hours before the match, manager Len Maddocks had denied a rumour that Thomson would play. As it eventuated, the selectors hadn't bothered to tell Maddocks. Thomson, whose ideas on his fitness were diametrically opposed to those of the pessimists, worked up extreme pace, reminding Dennis Amiss more than once that he had not lost the art of the bouncer. But neither Thomson, Malone or Walker took a wicket. Instead, it was the excruciatingly slow swing of Chappell and Cosier in the heavy atmosphere that accounted for all 10 England wickets.

At one stage, England was 7/90, but Old, 35, and Lever, 27 not out, hit sensibly in a 55 run stand that brought the total to

171. Chappell claimed 5/20 off 11 overs and Cosier 5/18 off 8.5. It seemed a reasonable target for the visitors, but again their batsmen blew the task comprehensively. From the second ball of the innings from Willis, which lifted sharply and was prodded into the gully by Davis, the Australians never came to terms with the situation. In a miserable total of 70, Chappell's 19 was the highest contribution and anybody who had fancied the Australians to hit their way out of trouble on this tour was fooling himself. As they had done from the beginning of the tour, most of the batsmen were sacrificing their wickets by attempting shots without moving their feet or adjusting backswing against the late moving delivery. Lever's opening spell of 4/14 made him the Man of the Match.

In fact, the only Australian victory in the last three days had come on 2 June when Kerry Packer, challenged on the David Frost Programme by *Sunday Times* cricket writer Robin Marlar and BBC television commentator Jim Laker, had emerged a clear winner. Marlar's truculence and inbuilt belief that Mr Packer was an Australian of below average-intelligence had cost his image dearly, especially as the audience was hand-picked for the occasion—'rent a crowd' it was called by some wag—and Frost was an old acquaintance of the rebels' leader. During the heated argument, Packer claimed it would not be his fault if his players' didn't continue to play Test cricket. 'I will bend over backwards to make them available—there will be no change to county cricket and there will be no change to Test cricket in England if we get together with the Board. If we don't get together with the Board, it's a different matter.' He omitted to mention that what he was really after was exclusive television rights to cricket in Australia.

Next day, 3 June, Mr Packer forecast on London radio that if the authorities did not negotiate with him in the first year of the Supertests, they probably would later. 'I don't want to administer cricket; I just want to give Australia a great series.'

And despite their feigned disinterest in the whole affair, I can vouch that the bar at the Australians' Manchester hotel emptied rapidly when word spread that Packer was on television. The Frost debate generated quick reaction. The noted cricket writer and commentator E. W. Swanton, in a letter to the *Daily Telegraph* said: 'The takings from Test cricket in all countries service the rest of first-class cricket and the game generally. By disrupting four tours in 1977–78, and 16 Test matches, how could Packer pretend that he would not be doing serious harm to international cricket?'

Author and former England spinner Ian Peebles wrote: ' . . . one effect of Mr Packer's venture, successful or otherwise, could be to deprive masses of poor people in poor countries of what they most cherish, their pride in the prowess of their own national cricket team'. And so the debate continued.

The Prudential Trophy, already won by England, concluded at The Oval on 6 June in extraordinary circumstances. Chappell, winning the toss for the third game in succession, again sent England in, and stood stoic-faced at first slip while Brearley, 78, and Amiss, 108, put on 161 for the first wicket after Brearley was missed at 23. The innings folded quickly after that, finishing at 242, a formidable task for the Australians, whose batting form had been lamentable, in extremely poor light and drizzle. McCosker was soon out for 11, but stop-gap opener Robinson and Chappell indulged themselves in a 148 run second wicket stand. Robinson, after a wand-waving start, settled down to play a responsible innings and to ensure for himself the Test place he craved so much. Chappell was at his best in appalling conditions. With 32 overs remaining, the rain came down by the bucketload and almost everyone went home. For reasons best known to themselves— or a bet—umpires Bird and Palmer decided to resume play when soccer officials might well have considered abandoning a fixture in such conditions. With the England bowlers ploughing through the mud, and Chappell trying hard to keep a straight and dry face, the farce was completed with Australia winning by two wickets.

There was a day to dry-out and then the tourists boarded an Aer Lingus jet for Dublin, a two-day game against Ireland, and 60 hours of laughs. Executives of Guinness Stout welcomed the party and whisked them straight to the brewery. The game itself was a draw, highlighted by a Serjeant hook on the first day that crashed through the bar room window, showering drinkers and cricketers—and one cricket writer—with glass. Amenities at the Leinster county ground, Dublin, aren't all they might be so the bar served as a bar, cafeteria, changing room, viewing room and press box. All the same, Mick Malone and Kerry O'Keeffe, allegedly 12th and 13th men for the game, put up a great exhibition to be still standing when the game ended in disarray.

A four-hour delay at Dublin airport made sure the Australians did not arrive at their Brentwood, Essex, hotel until dawn on 11 June, hardly satisfactory when the tourists' final game before the First Test was due to start at Chelmsford, 15 miles away, in less than seven hours. This type of itinerary must never again be accepted by Australian cricket authorities. This game was important, too, because on it the selectors had to judge the first Test prospects of Robinson, Serjeant, Hughes, Bright and O'Keeffe. At least four places in the side were wide open—a fast bowler, spinner, opening batsman, and number four batsman. A realist might have suggested another three places were open to doubt as the form of Walters, Hookes and McCosker had not been convincing.

Essex West Indian all-rounder Keith Boyce started the day off badly for the Australians, bowling Robinson and Serjeant for ducks. The first five wickets fell for 70, before Marsh, in his best innings to date, and Walters added 123. Marsh went on to 124 in Australia's total of 246 then the bowlers, in particular O'Keeffe, suffered miserably at the hands of South African Ken McEwan, who smashed 100 not out in 104 minutes, with four sixes, all off the leg-spinner, whose 75 runs came from only nine overs. Serjeant and Hookes redeemed themselves with second innings half-centuries as Marsh was forced to ignore the chance of a result in favour of badly needed practice for his batsmen.

England had announced its Jubilee Test 12 on the Sunday of this game with no real surprises. Kent right-hander Bob Woolmer had forced his way back with three county centuries after failing in the Centenary Test. The team was: M. Brearley (captain), D. Amiss, R. Woolmer, D. Randall, A. Greig, G. Barlow, A. Knott, C. Old, J. Lever, D. Underwood, R. Willis and G. Miller. Old had persuaded the selectors that he was fit, despite a shoulder injury he had suffered in a county game for Yorkshire a week earlier. Perhaps only Derbyshire's Mike Hendrick could feel disappointed, but as he had missed the tour to India and Australia the previous southern summer, he still had to oust one of the in-form pace bowlers, Willis, Lever and Old.

While the tourists tackled two days of practice at the Lord's nursery with some zest, the ubiquitous Mr Packer was not marking time either. His representatives were busy signing more top-class cricketers and on 13 June it was announced that England opening batsman Dennis Amiss, and West Indians Alvin Kallicharran and Collis King had signed. The official total now was 38, although it later became apparent that several other West Indians playing in England had also been recruited. Amiss' defection caused another shock wave in the Establishment; he had always been regarded as very much the staid and settled professional. When questioned, he gave the classic reply: 'It was an offer too good to refuse'.

Two days before the start of the Jubilee Test series, the ICC met in emergency session at Lord's to discuss the explosion that had split the cricket world. The six full and foundation members, Australia, England, India, Pakistan, West Indies and New Zealand were each represented by two delegates. The Australian pair, Board chairman Bob Parish and treasurer Ray Steele, were in London anyway as Test and County Cricket Board guests for the First Test. And they had spent many hours in unofficial talks with other delegates before the emergency session began. Australia, it was obvious, was to play the part of policy-maker in the ICC's deliberations. Most of the delegates felt that the affair affected Australia more than any other country and looked there for their lead.

When the seven-hour meeting ended, the Conference had decided it wanted to talk with Mr Packer after all. A short statement said simply: 'Mr Kerry Packer is being advised that should he wish to discuss his plans with representatives of the Test-match playing countries, a meeting will be arranged at the earliest convenient opportunity'. Mr Packer had, in fact, flown out of London only an hour earlier on his way back to Australia. He returned nine days later for the controversial meeting which formed the crux of the whole affair.

The offer to talk to Mr Packer looked, on face value, conciliatory. The impression given privately by ICC delegates was that it was not. The Australians, in particular, wanted to hear exactly what Mr Packer had in mind, but they were determined not to give ground. And the Sydney publishing and television chief was not under any illusions either. He felt, he admitted later, that the ICC was going to close the door on a compromise at any time.

Nevertheless, justice, even if it wasn't about to be done, at least had to appear to be done.

SIX

The cricketers, however, had other more pressing problems. The capricious English summer—for want of a better word—had turned nasty again, wiping out all chance of practice for the tourists on the day before the Test. Chappell, Marsh and Walters all had misgivings about the Lord's pitch, on which groundsman Jim Fairbrother had been forced to curtail his preparation. So the trio plumbed for a squad of 13, the final selection resting on a pitch inspection the next morning. The squad was: Chappell, Marsh, Bright, Hookes, O'Keeffe, Robinson, Serjeant, Pascoe, Malone, Walters, Walker, Thomson, McCosker. The alternatives were clear: either Pascoe or Malone would be the third fast bowler, and spinners O'Keeffe and Bright were still vying for one place. That squad must rank as one of the most inexperienced in Australian cricket since the Second World War. Five of the thirteen, Bright, Robinson, Pascoe, Malone and Serjeant had never played Test cricket and Hookes only once. Both Robinson and Serjeant were certain to play, as only six specialist batsmen were in the squad. Robinson had achieved his dearest wish—a Test cap—at the age of 30 after being overlooked on the domestic scene for several seasons. It had been his fighting 70 in the one-day game which finally got him there. Serjeant, too, deserved his place. He had played his first first-class game on 30 October the previous year, one of the fastest rises to Test match honours in Australian history. His batting in England on tour placed him second only to Chappell in consistency—six half-centuries in all tour games leading up to the Test. Both Davis and Cosier had surrendered their positions in the order by a series of indifferent performances in the lead-up games.

So the Jubilee Test began at Lord's on 16 June in fine, summer weather, a rarity for the character of 1977. It was the 226th Test match between the countries in 100 years of competition and Brearley got his captaincy away to a perfect start: he won the toss and elected to bat on a pitch that, despite all the prophets of doom, looked hard and fast, promising some help for the fast men and rewards for those batsmen prepared to graft and wait. An almost capacity crowd of 24,000 knew that off-spinner Geoff Miller had been made 12th man for England and left-arm spinner Bright and medium-pace bowler Malone left out of the Australian squad, giving Pascoe, at 27, his first chance in Test cricket. Ladbroke's, the betting people, had England slight favourites at 11/8 ahead of Australia 13/8, but the price setters had reason to change their minds after a few minutes. It seemed, then, that the pattern of the previous few encounters was to be continued. Thomson and his great mate Pascoe, in concert for the first time in a Test match, immediately tested England's openers Dennis Amiss and Mike Brearley.

Thomson started with a gentle full-toss which Amiss turned past short leg for 2, then settled quickly into his rhythm, the concern over his right arm and his run-up quickly evaporating. Pascoe was every bit as quick as his partner, although his tendency to pitch a trifle short brought Chappell sprinting from slip mid-way through his third over for a word of admonition. The game was only 37 minutes and 12 runs old when Amiss' susceptibility to extreme pace again cost him dearly. The right-hander had claimed early in the domestic season that he had worked out a new shuffling technique to counter the speed that had caused him so much embarrassment in the past. Evidently, the technique still needed adjustment as Amiss shuffled to a delivery of yorker length in Thomson's fifth over, misjudged the line and lost his off-stump. That was the last ball of the over. Brearley took a single from Walker who had come on from the pavilion end for Pascoe, then Thomson found himself on a hat-trick when the first delivery of his sixth over rose at Brearley's abdomen and the new captain could push it only gently into the waiting hands of Robinson, close in at short leg. So the man many said was finished, had captured

Amiss, 4, and Brearley, 9, in successive deliveries and England was 2/13. In the dressing room and in the press box, Australians relaxed. It was going to be a good summer after all!

Randall avoided the hat-trick as he withdrew bat and body from a nasty delivery that snaked past his eye-brows, then he and Bob Woolmer settled down to rehabilitate the innings. They got a bonus early in the battle when Chappell, still uncertain of his spearhead's fitness, rested Thomson at the completion of his sixth over. O'Keeffe was tested after 21 overs and 33 runs but it was soon obvious the slow men would be waiting a long time for any natural assistance. Woolmer, curbing his old tendency to flash at anything remotely short on or near the off-stump, was the epitome of the sheet-anchor. Randall, still riding high with the memory of his 174 in Melbourne in March, was the jaunty aggressor, once hooking Pascoe riskily over fine leg, to announce the first boundary of the series after 70 minutes and 16 overs. Walker, in his first spell, appeared to settle for a length slightly short of the requirement and at lunch, England had recovered to 2/63. The fifty partnership had come in an hour, and in the afternoon was carried to 98 in 125 minutes before Australia again tasted success. Randall was the trend-setter, appreciating the surprising bounce in the wicket by driving the fast bowlers repeatedly past point and cover. Once, he and Woolmer ran five from a pull shot that stopped just short of the boundary, causing the giant Walker, in full flight, to career over the boundary rope and get caught up in the Tavern crowd. Woolmer, on the other hand, was determined to eradicate that criticism which suggested he didn't have the stomach for a tough Test match fight. Randall brought up his half-century, nudging Pascoe through the slip field, in 114 minutes with 4 fours and a five, but his impetuosity then got the better of him. With the score 111, and his own contribution 53, he flung the bat needlessly at a wide delivery from Walker and Chappell clasped the ball happily into his midriff. It was the end of any concerted resistance to the Australian attack which, while not lethal, was attending to the job of containment assiduously.

Greig joined Woolmer at the wicket, after the MCC members had given him a reception that bordered on frosty silence. The tall South African, so recently hailed as the saviour of cricket in the old country, could hardly have been proud of his welcome from the Tavern and Mound stands either. He began with an adventurous drive at Walker, hard and waist-high, which just eluded an acrobatic catching effort by Walters at extra-cover, on its way to the boundary. But Greig only added another single before Len Pascoe made his day entirely miserable. The swarthy fast bowler, of Yugoslav parentage and a coalminer's physique, found an extra yard of pace that first struck Greig painfully on the chest, had a confident lbw appeal turned down and then sent the big man's off-stump bolting out of the ground. It was a fine piece of bowling and Pascoe fully deserved his first wicket in Test cricket. England was now struggling at 4/121 as the left-hander Barlow came in on his home ground, a question mark still against him as a Test batsman. He departed 25 minutes later for 1, having seen Woolmer to his half-century, but with the question mark still there. Walker, probing at his off-stump, induced a low edge, and although Barlow waited until Umpires Dicky Bird and Lloyd Budd conferred on the legitimacy of McCosker's catch at second slip, the decision was inevitable. England, tottering at 5/134 survived until tea through Woolmer, who showed more aggression after taking nearly three hours for his 50. The Kent right-hander still displayed a cast-iron defence but was more willing to produce a sweetly-timed off drive against the fast men. O'Keeffe gave him several moments of embarrassment, without quite producing the delivery to dismiss him.

England, 5/155 at tea, got another shock when the game resumed. Thomson loped in from the Nursery end for his customary loosener, a gentle half-volley which Alan Knott uncharacteristically ladled into the hands of Walters in the covers. The Australians could not conceal their delight and Knott, with time to review his slackness, must have known that he has never conceded to such a bad delivery. The tourists now had England on the run at 6/155 and gave new batsman Chris Old large doses of what he likes least: fast, short-pitched deliveries on the off-stump. Old played and missed several times, until he gambled once too often against Walker and the ever-alert Marsh was seen to toss the ball high into the air in a gesture that conveyed to all that he felt justice had been done. Old had contributed 9 to England's fast fading total of 7/171. Woolmer, fast running out of effective helpers, now felt inclined to take risks. He pushed Pascoe towards cover and decided to risk the reflexes of Doug Walters, who accepted the challenge, scooped up the ball and raced towards the non-striker's end. Just when it seemed Woolmer would win the race, Walters under-handed the ball unerringly and England was 8/183. Woolmer's 79 had taken him 270 minutes and included 7 fours, but more importantly showed him now as a mature, if not exciting, number three England player. When Pascoe bowled Lever off his pads for 8—his second wicket of the innings—England was 9/189 and only two batsmen Randall and Woolmer, had reached double figures. That the last pair, Underwood and Willis, were able to do so with intelligent hitting was an indictment of their more esteemed fellows. Their stand of 27 in 37 minutes was to prove of immense value later in the game when Australia wanted quick runs to win.

When Thomson finally ended proceedings, yorking the big-swinging Willis for 17, England had reached 216 all out. Thomson returned the best figures of 4/41 off 20.5 overs, ample evidence of his form and fitness but Pascoe, 2/53 off 23 overs, had been the more impressive, sustaining his pace over long periods and showing a willingness to watch and learn his art at the highest level. With no time left for Australia to bat, the tourists had a night to savour a commanding situation.

Friday dawned dull and drizzly, a complete contrast to the summer fare of the first day, and only 104 minutes of play was possible. Then, on a pitch assisting the bowlers, Australia struggled to reach 51 for the loss of Richie Robinson, who opened the batting in preference to Serjeant. Play started 75 minutes late with Willis leading off proceedings to the debutant Robinson, who swung suicidally at the first delivery. Defence has never been the outstanding characteristic of the Victorian captain's batting and he obviously wasn't going to change his style now. He took his first run from Willis' second delivery, turning him off the hip for a single, and soon produced a mighty square drive for four off Lever. But in the heavy atmosphere and with the ball moving off the moistened pitch,

42

Robinson's end was always nigh. McCosker, infected by his partner's mood, got early runs off both Willis and Lever, the pair adding 25 in 24 minutes. Then Robinson, driving at Lever, was beaten badly and his stumps shattered. His contribution of 11 could hardly be said to have been the answer to Australia's opening problems.

Greg Chappell came onto the ground where he had scored a century in his first Lord's Test appearance in 1972 and was immediately striking the ball firmly in his cool, correct, straight-backed style. Brearley introduced the left-arm spin of Derek Underwood after only eight overs, wishing more than anticipating that the rain which had already fallen on the pitch would suit the Kent man. There was little in his first six overs that could be construed as dangerous but McCosker and Chappell took only four runs in that time.

Forty minutes after lunch, the players were forced from the field when light rain added to the murk. They were back again in 20 minutes, but finally departed at 3.25 p.m. when light rain started again. By then, McCosker and Chappell had laboured to 1/51, the 50 coming in 99 minutes off 23.3 overs. It wasn't entertaining, but the batsmen were forced to defend in the most trying conditions and the Australians could feel happy enough about their position. It was some time before umpires Bird and Budd finally decreed play finished for the day and under the strange English law of cricket, the pitch was left uncovered between the creases. This, said the pundits in no uncertain fashion, meant Underwood would be unplayable in the morning.

McCosker, 23 not out and Chappell, 13, must have been suspecting the same situation when they resumed on Saturday morning. Randall was off the ground for England, suffering a strange malaise of the left arm which produced a large, red swelling and rendered it useless. X-rays had revealed no fracture; later the doctors decided he had bursitis. His place was taken by the burly Kent batsman Alan Ealham, revered in the county game as a fieldsman of great skill and unbounding energy, now on the field for England under a commonsense agreement that allowed the 12th man to undertake county duties during the week-end of any Test match. It is remarkable and ironical that a logical rule is employed in one area, and an antiquated one on the covering of pitches is still used in another.

It was Old, not Underwood, who made the initial break-through on this the third day. Without a run added, McCosker pushed forward to the seventh ball of the morning. It cut back sharply between bat and pad and knocked out the Australian opener's middle stump, sending him unhappily to the pavilion for 23. Australia, now 2/51, faced a testing time. Serjeant, although the form batsman of the party, was facing a tight attack in trying conditions in his first Test match, but a compensation was the presence of his captain at the other end. Chappell almost wasn't there for long. With only three runs added, he drove at Underwood without getting to the pitch and the England players were stunned to see the bowler put down a straightforward chance. Chappell, two runs earlier, had almost played on to the same bowler but, sensing his luck was in, decided the day was his. Serjeant, capless and very nervous, went through trauma before he scored his first run. He played and missed several times to Old and his slightly cross-batted style was discovering problems against Underwood that had never before been apparent. It took the dark-haired Western Australian pharmacist 39 minutes and 32 deliveries before he turned Old through mid-wicket for that vital first run. His confidence soared quickly enough for him to swing Under-wood over mid-wicket for his first boundary after 50 minutes, and soon enough he was repeating the shot to a rare loose delivery. That was enough frivolity and Serjeant retreated back into his defensive shell, sweating through another runless half hour before he again found the nerve to sweep Underwood for four.

With the light fading, Chappell, too, was watchful and in the two hours until lunch, advanced his score from 11 to 39. Then it was 1/99 with Serjeant 17. Underwood had bowled for 100 minutes in this session, and while his pinpoint accuracy kept the batsmen at times motionless, there was little assistance for him from the pitch. His 12 overs had yielded only 23 runs before Brearley brought Willis back from the pavilion end.

Only 13 minutes after lunch, the umpires decided the light

was too bad. Chappell had advanced to 48, Serjeant was 19 and Australia 2/110. Slow hand-claps had indicated that the long-suffering capacity house wanted more than the tense fight they were getting and Chappell had attempted to oblige with two powerful drives straight after the break. Another 30 minutes was lost, which, added to the 256 minutes lost on Friday, was quickly dimming the hopes of either side for a positive result. Chappell reached his half-century in the first over from Willis after the interruption. It had taken him a marathon 212 minutes with only a single boundary, but the Australian captain was providing an example to his young charges, and Serjeant was following his lead admirably. Now Chappell's mood changed abruptly. He went onto the back-foot to unleash a powerful square drive that almost made old Father Time smile as it smashed into the wall below him. Chappell raced to 66 with two more boundaries, a cover drive and a hook off Willis, then was punished for his aggression. Still looking for the drive, he got a thick edge which travelled quickly into the hands of Old in the gully. Chappell's 66 had taken him 230 minutes with 4 fours, and Australia at 3/135 now stood at the crossroads.

Walters, whose quicksilver reflexes have made him a great batsman on quick wickets, has never quite come to terms with the game in England. On Walters' fourth visit, Chappell was looking to him for vastly-improved displays as the tourists' most senior batsman. The Chappell-Serjeant partnership of 84 in 150 minutes had set a perfect foundation for him and Walters proceeded with aggression. Brearley greeted him with three slips and two gullies—by now a customary field for a man who has so often been caught in that arc in England—but Walters was unperturbed. Serjeant was batting in pain from a bad gash on his right shin—the legacy of a fielding mishap in Dublin—and which John Lever unkindly aggravated when a delivery hit Serjeant's pad. But he had got the message from Walters: attack, attack! And attack he did, producing one superb hook off Old, a powerful blow that convinced the fast bowler to re-direct his line. Walters, of course, had his luck. At 21, he offered a simple chance to Brearley at first slip, but the England captain unsighted himself, moving the wrong way and

45

barely getting his hands to what should have been a straightforward dismissal. The 50 partnership between the pair came in even time, then Serjeant turned Willis off his legs to bring up the milestone of his first Test half-century in 205 minutes with 5 fours.

Brearley took the new ball shortly after tea, with Australia 3/213 and immediately Serjeant cover-drove Lever for three to level the scores. He put Australia in the lead, driving Willis' first delivery with the new ball for four and moving confidently to 65. Walters, when he reached 27, achieved a personal milestone of his own. In four Tests at cricket headquarters, it was his highest score, eclipsing his efforts of 26 and 0 in 1968, 1 in 1972 and 2 in 1975. Serjeant was now all classical stroke maker, pulling Willis high over mid-wicket and on-driving Lever superbly to the fence at the Nursery end of the ground. The next went through slips for four and the next hurtled back past the bowler for another four. 'Go easy, son', Ian Chappell was heard to mutter in the press box, but the words of warning came too late. Serjeant added another single to go to 81 then assayed the wildest of cuts at a wide Willis delivery. The ball took the under-edge and Knott, moving low to his right, held it high for all to see. It was a pity such an impetuous act had cost Serjeant his chance of a maiden Test hundred, after four hours and 17 minutes of well-mixed grind and aggression which had yielded 10 boundaries.

Australia, at least, was now well-placed at 4/238 to go to a healthy lead, but Bob Willis had other ideas. His approach to the wicket—and the game—had improved rapidly under the combined efforts of Tony Greig and Mike Brearley and he was about to show the Australians that the Willis of old—fast for five overs then barely sighted again—was gone forever. First, however, Walters reached his half-century in 117 minutes with 7 fours. Then he leant forward to leg-glance Willis, but somehow deflected the ball from his pad in a gentle arc to Brearley at slip. While everyone stood bemused, Walters left the scene, long before umpire Lloyd Budd could confirm the appeal. For once the enigmatic Walters looked thoroughly disappointed.

From 5/256, Australia quickly slumped. Only eight runs

were added before David Hookes prodded at a rising delivery from Old and Brearley pocketed his second catch with nonchalance. Hookes, 10, was followed to the pavilion one run later by Rod Marsh, who pushed forward to Willis, missed and hardly needed a signal from Mr Budd to know his fate—lbw for 1, Australia 7/265. Willis, then, had brought his side back into the game, capturing Serjeant, Walters and Marsh for a personal cost of five runs in 30 deliveries. Max Walker and Kerry O'Keeffe held on grimly until stumps were drawn three minutes early, again because of the bad light. By then, Australia was 7/278, a lead of 62 runs with two days' play remaining.

If the Australians had reason to be happy with the state of the world on Saturday night, they were red-faced with anger on Sunday morning. For when they picked up their editions of the *Sunday Mirror*, they read that former England captain Ted Dexter was accusing Len Pascoe of throwing. There is no nastier accusation in the game. Apart from the bodyline era— and some still say Harold Larwood had a suspect action— there has been no uglier period in its evolution than the late fifties and early sixties when a bevy of chuckers on the first-class scene were weeded out by the authorities. Dexter, in his weekly column, stated emphatically that Pascoe had thrown his fastest deliveries when bowling on the previous Thursday, his first day of Test cricket.

Dexter said: 'Camera evidence on slow-motion television replays offers unquestionable proof that he is an occasional thrower'. However, Dexter waited until the 31st paragraph of his column before he could bring himself to say, 'the crucial symptom is Pascoe's left foot, which splays out, opening the shoulders and making any kind of fast ball an almost certain throw. Among other signs last Thursday was the way little-known Pascoe outpaced Jeff Thomson from the start, bowling a more effective bouncer and, even more damning, lost his usual ability to swing the ball away.'

His reasoning was circumstantial to say the least. On those grounds, anyone who bowled faster than Thomson automatically became a suspect. To my mind, it was Fleet Street hypocrisy at its worst. Almost as if his editor had said, 'Hey,

47

Ted, you haven't said anything controversial for all that money we are paying you. Stir something up'. Pascoe's action had been described during the Test, by no less a person than Richie Benaud, as a perfect model for any aspiring young fast bowler. He generated his pace from a bullocking run-up and a full twist of his strong shoulders in the delivery stride. Dexter finished off his article by suggesting that umpires Bird and Budd give Pascoe a thorough inspection during the second innings. At least, it can never be said that the umpires don't read their newspapers. They did give him a thorough inspection, and Dicky Bird took the unprecedented step of going to the Australian dressing room at the completion of the Test to say his action was regarded by them as faultless.

Still, the reaction among the Australians was one of anger. Greg Chappell swore for several seconds when asked for a comment, then replied, 'I'm not going to comment on garbage like that'. Manager Len Maddocks pointed out that Pascoe's action had never before been questioned in England or Australia. Pascoe himself was bemused then decided to treat the matter as a joke. 'I'll put my arm in a splint', he offered good-humouredly.

The big New South Welshman had not even expected to play in this Test—or any other. Now he found himself the centre of controversy over his tireless bowling. Early in the tour, Pascoe had given Greg Chappell a lesson in the art of his appetite for work. Chappell, in a county game, had let him bowl eight overs at top pace. Then he asked Pascoe how he felt. 'What do you mean, am I tired?' bellowed Pascoe. 'I came here to bowl and that's what I'll do, tired or not.'

'Alright', said a surprised Chappell, 'I won't ask you again'. He didn't either.

The furore grew rapidly on Sunday—the rest day—then Dexter really put his foot in it by suggesting on BBC television on Monday morning that Bob Willis threw too. By then, too many people were laughing out loud for his statements to have much credence.

Willis took only 54 minutes to wrap up the Australian innings when play resumed on time on the fourth morning. He had Walker caught by Alan Knott for 4, tempted O'Keeffe into hooking high to substitute Alan Ealham for 12, then bowled Thomson for six to finish off the innings at 296, a lead of 80. His final analysis of 7/78 off 30.1 overs was his best in Test cricket, eclipsing his 6/53 against India at Bangalore in February.

Nearly an hour before lunch, England began its task of saving the game disastrously. With the weather still cold and miserable, Thomson did his best to warm Australian hearts. Dennis Amiss played right inside the line of his fourth delivery of the innings and was bowled for a duck, England 1/0. Then came the first signs of the disease that was to afflict the Australians for the rest of the series and make their monumental task of winning impossible. Not a chance had been missed on the first day. From now on, however, nothing seemed to stick. Bob Woolmer joined Brearley and both had early lives that were to prove embarrassingly expensive. The pair took the score sedately to 1/29 at lunch, neither much troubled by Thomson, Pascoe or Walker, who was into the attack after seven overs. But at 39, both were dropped. First, Brearley prodded a nasty Thomson delivery away from his ribs and Robinson, diving desperately from short leg, got it in his hands, only to see the ball fall out. Brearley was then 19 and was to add another 30. In Walker's next over, Woolmer, 20, edged Walker into the gully where Craig Serjeant, a brilliant fieldsman in Australia, put down what he should have held. Woolmer added another 100 runs to his tally. Nonetheless, the English pair did an admirable job of saving the match. Brearley, with his plastic headguard as a token to his respect of Thomson's pace, is a man of strictly limited capacity but he plays carefully within that capacity. This day he did so for nearly three hours and 49 runs in a partnership of 132 with Woolmer. Woolmer, the first-innings top scorer, was much more confident, and prepared to display early in his innings his penchant for the drive and square cut. Often he played and missed, especially at Walker and Pascoe but the thin edge was avoided. Both batsmen survived confident lbw appeals by Max Walker and the fire of Pascoe and Thomson early did nothing for their confidence. Pascoe seemed unaffected by the actions of the ostentatious Mr Bird who went to point to observe the fast bowler's first two overs after lunch. In one of them, Pascoe

49

sent down four short pitched deliveries at Brearley, before Bird, returned, satisfied, to square-leg.

After 24 overs, Chappell came on himself for the luckless Thomson but the English pair were well-established. The 50 partnership had come in 80 minutes and the century partnership followed as a matter of course in 134 minutes. It wasn't until seven minutes before tea that Brearley leaned forward to O'Keeffe, a late introduction to the attack, and the ever-present Robinson snapped him up low at short-leg. Despite his first innings failure—and the missing of Brearley at 19—Robinson had been a decided asset to Australia in the field and his alertness in this dismissal merely emphasized that.

Although Woolmer, now 76 not out, had been the dominant partner in the 132 run partnership, Brearley had given his answer to the critics who claimed he wasn't good enough for a Test spot. Woolmer had reached his half-century in 125 minutes with a series of hooks off Pascoe, and now proceeded to show the way to his new partner, the ambitious Greig. Woolmer, reached his century shortly before stumps in 219 minutes with 12 fours, 51 minutes quicker than it had taken him over his first innings 79. It was his second 100 against Australia, the first being in that dreary Fourth Test at The Oval in 1975 when he earned the dubious honour of scoring the slowest century in Anglo-Australian Test matches. Since then, it was said, his batting had not progressed. This day's evidence was to the contrary. Greig, perhaps sensing that his place could be in jeopardy in the changing climate of English thought, was prepared to take a back seat as Woolmer continued to press the attack for runs. By stumps, England was 2/189 with Woolmer 114 and Greig 18 and the Jubilee Test all but over as a contest. Or so we thought.

England began the last, overcast day, with a lead of 109 and little inclination to chase quick runs, pending a challenging declaration by Brearley. Only 35 runs came in the first 50 minutes, and of these Woolmer could manage only six. Greig's confidence was growing as it rapidly became apparent that the pitch, instead of deteriorating, had become more placid under the several showers of rain it had received. By the time Woolmer prodded forward to Pascoe and gave Chappell an easy slip catch, England was 3/224 and cruising in safe waters. Woolmer's stay of five hours, five minutes had yielded 120 runs, with 13 fours, and had achieved its target of keeping the Australian bowlers at bay. Chappell's reaction in throwing down the stumps as Woolmer departed was the Australian captain's reaction to an innings which often had the slips cordon gasping in frustration as a tentative bat just missed deliveries from the pace trio. Greig celebrated Graham Barlow's arrival at the wicket by bringing up his own half-century in 145 minutes with 5 fours. Chappell called on the new ball immediately it was due at 3/224 after 85 overs, but Greig was able to quicken the pace, employing his long reach to good effect in a series of drives against Thomson and Walker. Barlow, never at ease, nonetheless held on grimly, making 5 in a stand of 39 with Greig. At 263, he was fourth man out as Pascoe trapped him in two minds and only his back pad stopped the ball from taking his middle stump. There was still no sign that this Test would end in anything but a tame draw. Alan Knott, missed at 6 by Max Walker, helped Greig advance the score to 286.

And then, the Jubilee Test rose from the dead. Greig, suddenly abandoned the discretion which had guided him to 91 invaluable runs in 225 minutes and sliced a wide delivery from Pascoe straight and knee-high to O'Keeffe in the gully. With the first ball of the last over before lunch, Knott followed his former captain's example and slashed irresponsibly at Walker and Walters, in the covers, accepted the catch. So England went to lunch at 6/286 and if its position in the last few minutes had become shaky, it could blame two of its most experienced players.

Walker resumed after the 40 minute break and with his fourth delivery grabbed the vital wicket of Old, who cut it straight to Walters forward of point. The Australians were now scenting a chance for victory, which grew stronger with the third ball of Thomson's next over, the second after lunch. Randall, batting under difficulties because of the bursitis in his left arm, edged the Australian speedster, McCosker leapt forward and held an exciting catch in his left hand only inches from the ground. Neither Old nor Randall had scored, and

England was 8/286, losing its last four wickets for no runs in the space of 11 deliveries.

With the large crowd suddenly galvanized by the realization that the Test was once more a contest, John Lever and Derek Underwood tackled the task of regaining lost ground. For 26 invaluable minutes and 19 priceless runs, they held on, taking England past the 300 mark in 433 minutes of 111.1 overs. At 2.40 p.m., Thomson induced Lever to jab at a short-pitched delivery and Marsh took the catch. Willis fell the same way to the next delivery and the innings was over at 305, with Underwood 12 not out. The last six England wickets had fallen for only 19 runs and Australia, needing 226 runs in 105 minutes and 20 overs, undeniably had a chance to snatch a remarkable victory. Good catching and the pace bowling of Thomson, Pascoe and Walker had given them that chance. Thomson again had the best figures—4/86 off 24.4 overs—giving him a match haul of 8/127. Did someone say he was unfit?

Robinson left no one in doubt about Australia's intentions. He mis-hit Willis high over the slips cordon in the first over for a boundary, in full knowledge that Australia needed a breezy start from him to make a reality of its ambitions. Chris Old, who opened from the pavilion end, had other ideas. In his first over, Robinson went on to the back foot and turned him straight into the hands of Woolmer at short-leg. It was Old's 100th victim in 32 Test matches and made it a day of personal milestones. Rod Marsh's dismissal of Willis to end the England innings was his 70th victim in Tests against that country, breaking the old standard set by the late Wally Grout.

But victory, not records, was on the minds of both sides now. Brearley, by his attacking pose, obviously felt that the Australians could lose this match if they played recklessly. There was nothing reckless, however, about the forward defensive shot that brought about McCosker's demise from the first ball of Willis' second over. It was the perfect off-cutter which spread-eagled McCosker's stumps for the second time in the match. Australia, at 2/5, could well have been forgiven for abandoning thoughts of the chase; but Chappell had made up his mind and wasn't about to change it. David Hookes was in at number 4, again giving a clue to the thoughts going on in the

52

dressing room. The natural stroke-play of the 22-year-old South Australian left-hander was far more suited to quick runs than the more dour style of Serjeant, who had batted there in the first innings. Chappell himself was intent on using his great talents to their fullest in the cause. He and Hookes added 43 runs in 40 minutes by dint of shrewd hitting against Willis and Old who conceded 48 runs in the first 10 overs. So the tourists were roughly on target when Chappell's ambitious hook at Old over-reached the bounds of discretion. The ball sailed high into the air and Lever, running around from wide mid-on made ground to make a difficult chance look easy. Australia's hopes effectively ended there but Walters was in no mood to believe that. After 10 runs, he swung rashly at Underwood and was easily caught behind square leg by substitute Alan Ealham, his second catch of the match. At 4/64, Australia could safely be described as now fighting for survival, a position Craig Serjeant failed to realize. He troubled the bowling for only three runs before he, too, swiped inconclusively at Underwood and Amiss at mid-on accepted the catch.

At 5/71, Australia now needed resolute defence to save the game, yet another transformation in a match that had seemed destined for a draw for so long. The bookmakers that morning had offered 16/1 Australia, 12/1 England and 1/10 the draw; by tea-time their pencils were worn down, so often and wildly had the odds fluctuated. At tea, Australia had seemed safe at 3/64, now Hookes and Marsh were engaged in a battle of grim defence against the sheer consistency of Underwood and the occasional swerve of Willis and Old. Still, Hookes was equal to the task although early in his innings he was beaten repeatedly by the pace bowlers. As his defence improved, so did his confidence, enough for him to sweep Underwood for six. With the final 20 overs begun, Hookes reached his half-century, then lost his wicket as he gave Willis an easy return catch. And television viewers on both sides of the Equator needed only a basic knowledge of lip-reading to know what young Mr Hookes thought about that shot. Australia, 6/102, wasn't quite clear of danger yet, but Marsh and O'Keeffe, two old hands at no-nonsense defence, saw out the peril. When play ceased with five of the 20 overs still remaining, Australia was 6/114, still 112 runs short of victory. Only fleetingly, when Chappell was at the wicket, had they looked capable of the challenge. England, on the other hand, was probably marginally closer to victory when it had half the side out for 71.

Still, the Jubilee Test had ended in an honourable draw. Both sides could afford to be reasonably happy with the result while the rest of us were left to ponder what might have been if most of Friday and a half hour on Saturday had not been lost to the rain and light.

Lessons were there to be learned on both sides. The tourists knew now that Thomson was probably fitter than most of them had believed he could possibly be; that in Pascoe they had unearthed a strong and willing fast bowler—who, in the right conditions, would test any batting line-up. The two young batsmen, Serjeant and Hookes, had both made significant contributions under extreme pressure. On the debit side, both opening batting positions were a continuing source of worry. Robinson, despite his enthusiasm, was plainly not the answer and McCosker still appeared edgy and out of form. And if O'Keeffe was the best of the country's slow bowlers, the purveyors of speed were in for a series of hard work. The catching, too, needed much work. Three chances had been put down in England's second innings, two of them allowing Brearley and Woolmer to build a match-saving partnership.

England's selectors must have been happiest with the new determination and character of Bob Woolmer. Two seasons ago, he had often batted at number 8 or number 9 for his county Kent. Now, after 24 months of topsy-turvy form, his innings of 79 and 120 had established him as his country's number three batsman. The new image of lanky fast bowler Bob Willis had been another great boost for the side. Willis had worked hard on his fitness and his run-up during and after the winter tour to India and Australia and his nine wickets in this match were a fine reward. Chris Old, too, had bowled well, reinforcing the opinion that many judges in England held: that he was the most effective medium-pace bowler in the land. There were problems, of course. Amiss had done nothing in this game to overcome the nagging fear that he was not capable of handling Test-class fast bowling. Graham Barlow was another batsman who had failed to make ground in the selectors' eyes, and the left-arm of John Lever in this match had not been nearly as effective as expected.

With all that said, those who were at Lord's for the Jubilee Test walked out of the ground almost convinced that captains Greg Chappell and Mike Brearley had previewed the series correctly: that the two teams were evenly matched.

SEVEN

While most of the tourists spent 22 June basking in the hot sun and brilliant tennis of the Centenary Wimbledon tournament, officials of the International Cricket Conference countries were formulating their policy for the meeting with Kerry Packer the next day.

During the Jubilee Test, West Indian opening batsman Gordon Greenidge confirmed that he had joined the troupe. The official count was 40, although Mr Packer said in London that he had now 51 players on his books. But the promoters were not in the mood to release the full list. There was also a report from Australia that John Maley, the young Brisbane Cricket Ground curator who had joined the troupe to take charge of the preparation of wickets, was returning to his former employer. Whatever the truth behind that, Maley stayed on with the new group.

Mr Packer arrived for the momentous meeting at Lord's in a chaffeur-driven limousine with an entourage of David McNicoll, a director of the Packer publishing company, Australian Consolidated Press; Lynton Taylor, an executive of the Packer television company, TCN 9; and Richie Benaud, in his capacity as a Packer sporting adviser. Two and a quarter hours later, Packer emerged from the committee room an angry man.

The meeting had foundered on his demand for exclusive television rights to cricket in Australia after the 1978–79 season, when the Australian Broadcasting Commission's current agreement with the Australian Cricket Board expired. This, quite plainly, was not an agreement that the ICC could undertake; one country's television arrangements are a

56

domestic matter nowhere near the jurisdiction or even consideration of the international body. During the meeting there had been agreement between the parties on five major matters, matters which very nearly resulted in a spectacular compromise that could have completely revolutionized the face of cricket in one afternoon.

The points put to Mr Packer by the ICC's emergency committee were:

1 The programme and grounds of the Packer games to be acceptable to the home authority and the duration of the Packer season to be six weeks, unless otherwise agreed. The matches to be under the control of the home authority and played in accordance with the laws of cricket.

2 No player to participate in these games without the permission of his home authority. This permission would not be withheld unreasonably.

3 No teams taking part in these matches to be represented as national teams. Instead of 'Australia', it would have to be an Australian XI, or something similar.

4 Players contracted to Mr Packer to be available for Test matches, first-class matches and other home authority-sponsored matches where there is no clash.

5 The home authority to be able to honour all contractual commitments to existing sponsors and advertisers.

After hearing these conditions, Mr Packer declared that none of them provided insurmountable problems and proposed a working committee, or series of committees, to debate them. So, surprisingly, there was wide ground for compromise . . . until Mr Packer told the meeting of his two points. He wanted a complete guarantee from the ICC that there would be no victimization of any of the players who had signed with him, and he wanted the exclusive TV rights. The last came as no surprise to most of the ICC members, who had been forewarned of Mr Packer's rabid interest in securing exclusivity of cricket on his Australian Channel 9 network. There was a brief intermission, while the Sydney television mogul had his first glimpse of the famous cricket ground. Then the meeting resumed and ICC chairman Mr W. H. 'Tadge' Webster said: 'It is the unanimous decision of the ICC that they will not grant television rights in advance'. According to Mr Packer's version of the meeting, he then suggested that the question of television rights be included on the agenda of the working committee. Mr Webster replied that this was not acceptable and the meeting was over.

Outside the room, Mr Packer faced a barrage of questions from journalists. It was obvious from his answers that cricket was now in a state of emergency: the compromise that had been the wish of many of those involved in the breakaway was now a fading hope. There would be many losers before the two parties eventually got together, but none bigger than the game itself.

'I will now take no steps to help anyone, every man for himself and the devil take the hindmost. I compromised so much that I felt strange in myself. I thought we were going to reach a period of breakthrough but the talks failed because of the stubbornness of the ICC', said Mr Packer. 'I have never wanted to control cricket, but I wanted and I would have expected to get exclusive rights when the current TV contracts ran out.'

ICC secretary Mr Jack Bailey countered with: 'Any guarantee of TV rights at any time would be against cricket's best interests . . . You do not enter into agreements for three years time and [you] don't accept conditions that let down other TV companies . . . The other countries, apart from Australia, are not particularly interested in the fact that the ABC network has televised cricket well in Australia, but the principle is interesting to them . . . We thought he was prepared to compromise but there was no possibility of that once this television area had been entered into.'

Despite the claims of both sides that they had bent over backwards to reach a compromise, I don't believe either had planned it that way. The ICC, swayed heavily by Australian reaction to the troupe, knew that the television rights question was vital to Mr Packer. After all, he had already had two attempts to get the rights defeated by the Australian Cricket Board. The five points submitted by the emergency committee were done so in the knowledge that the whole meeting hinged on the one question. Yet it is surprising that compromise came so close with Mr Packer's agreement on those points. It is probably easy to say with the benefit of hindsight, but Mr Packer could have established then and there his troupe's influence on the future of the game if he had insisted on the guarantee of no harassment of his players and shelved the question of television rights until the end of the 1978–79 season. By that time, the rebel troupe would have had 2 six-week seasons in Australia—televised exclusively by Channel 9, naturally—and those seasons would have been run under the auspices of the controlling body of international cricket, the ICC. Not only would he and his cricketers have won a much larger measure of public support, it is feasible that the idea of exclusivity of television rights could have been accepted in that time by the ACB. And Mr Packer's determination to get those rights had been so apparent, he was going to bid as much as was needed to get them.

As it was, Mr Packer and his advisers were well aware that the ICC was in no position to grant exclusive rights for games played in a member country. And it must be stressed that his total preoccupation with the television question, and his admitted readiness to hand over control of the troupe's proposed games, pointed strongly to the Establishment's contention that Mr Packer was involved in a domestic ratings battle, rather than a desire to change the concept of the game because of the dissatisfaction of the players.

Now the battle lines were drawn. Despite the willingness of the West Indies to go along with the Packer troupe if it did not affect the proposed tour by Australia early in 1978, it was now clear that the ICC would take a hard line against the signatories when it met in its annual session at Lord's on 26 and 27 July. As the commentator and writer E. W. Swanton said in the August edition of *Cricket International*: '. . . they [the ICC] were willing to accept the intrusion of a six-week programme into the Australian summer and take responsibility for its control: in fact, to legitimize the bastard child despite the sordid circumstances of its conception.'. Now, that child was to be ostracized.

There was certainly no suggestion that Mr Packer and his revolutionaries had been caught short by the breakdown of the talks. Plans for the main series, and the associated games, were

59

well advanced. A company, J. P. Sport Pty Ltd, had been formed to act as the promoter. At its inception the company had a paid-up capital of 98 $1 shares, held as follows: TCN 9—49 shares, John Cornell—16 shares, Paul Hogan—16 shares, Austin Robertson—15 shares, Kerry Packer—2 shares. The paid-up share capital of the company was later to become an important point of legal discussion as some players made efforts to dissociate themselves from the troupe.

The promoters claimed they had the use of grounds in every capital city in Australia, although it was known that approaches to use the Melbourne Cricket Ground and the Adelaide Oval had been turned down. For a long time, many of the people connected with the Packer troupe, including Mr Packer, claimed that the idea was not born until early in 1977. No one has yet explained the revelation by Melbourne Cricket Club secretary, and former Australian captain, Ian Johnson that he received a letter in September 1976, seeking permission to use the MCG in December, January and February of the 1977–78 season for a series of matches. The letter came from GTV 9, the Melbourne channel of the Nine network, controlled by Mr Packer. With the two sides now facing each other across barbed-wire entanglements it was unlikely that the cricket Establishment in Australia would concede the rebels use of any of the normal first-class cricket venues. And so it was that on 30 June, Mr Packer announced that three of his troupe's matches in the coming summer would be played at VFL Park, Melbourne—or more correctly, about 15 miles out of Melbourne, in the outer suburb of Waverley where the Victorian Football League had invested $20 million in a vast stadium that it had hoped would take over from the MCG as the mecca of Australian football. Never, never, never, the VFL had promised over the years, would the ground be used for cricket. The two sports have never been close friends in Australia, especially in Melbourne. But every man, or football league, has its price and $825,000 for the use of the stadium for a limited period each summer for three years was the VFL's price, despite vigorous lobbying by the Victorian Cricket Association. 'We need the money', was the simple explanation of VFL officials, as the Packer organization began building a greenhouse just outside the stadium which was to become the nursery of a revolutionary method of producing cricket wickets. In that greenhouse, artificially heated and under the constant glare of 80 special lamps, curator John Maley was attempting to produce a series of wickets that could be transported to different grounds to be used in the matches. Now the sparring was over. No one on either side was pretending that the game had not been split into bitterly-divided camps. And there was every indication that the split would widen and become more bitter in the ensuing months. Mr Packer made no secret of his plans. In Sydney on 30 June, he promised an 'all out scrap' if any of his players was banned from playing international, county or interstate cricket. 'There will be retaliation if this happens', he promised and went on to outline what he meant by retaliation. The troupe would come to England and play matches there. There would be a direct confrontation with established cricket in Australia in the summer of 1977–78; the Supertests would be scheduled in the same cities and at the same times as the five Test matches between Australia and India. As well, said Mr Packer, players under contract to him would be forming an organization aimed at allowing professional cricketers to take over the running of the series.

He went on to deny reports from England that some players were having second thoughts about their decision to sign contracts to play in the troupe. He was slightly awry there. Quite a number of the Australian tourists were having second thoughts. It was no secret to those journalists travelling with the party that several of the younger players were spending many hours discussing the strengths and weaknesses of the troupe and its plans. And as the enormity of the impending battle began to hit home, several of them began to look for a way out. Although, without exception, the signatories claimed they had known they faced expulsion from Test and Sheffield Shield ranks before they signed, the difference between awareness and experience was starting to become rather frightening to them. Some—Ian Davis, David Hookes, Ray Bright, Mick Malone, Len Pascoe—were being subjected to enormous pressure, pressure that no earlier tourists had ever known. On one hand, the older players kept reassuring them that they had made the right move, that cricket as they knew it now could not promise the riches and opportunity offered by Mr Packer. On the other, representatives of the Establishment, and those of us not convinced that the rebellion was good for the game, were urging a return to the fold. Such confusion was hardly the sort of atmosphere in which a young touring cricket team could hope to perform at its best.

There was not much doubt that the official reaction of the International Cricket Conference, and the Test and County Cricket Board would be to press for a ban on the Packer players. The TCCB had called a meeting for 15 July to decide its policy, which would be passed on to the ICC which was to convene on 26 July. A majority of the 17 counties had already indicated they would be calling for a ban from both Test and county cricket for the players.

The feeling in England was that the Packer plans threatened the very existence of the county competition. The present financial position of some of the counties is weak to say the least. It is estimated that the TCCB supplies about 40 per cent of the income of the counties annually and this money comes from home Test match series. The major money-spinners, of course, are the series against Australia and the West Indies. If the Supertests went ahead and became successful, public interest in the official Test matches would be less—and the money available to the counties correspondingly less. Even in the event of a compromise between the factions, the amount of money available generally to cricket and its upkeep would be diminished.

The reaction of Australian authorities was rather more personal, with less concern for the danger to the welfare of the game. Some senior Australian officials took the Packer troupe's existence as a personal affront. Indeed, two of them, on first hearing the news, had called for the instant return of the touring team from England. Thankfully, wiser counsel prevailed. Still, the general Australian attitude was hardline: the rebels must not be allowed to disrupt the normal procedures and administration of cricket. And Australia was prepared to put pressure on the West Indies, the only full ICC member who

seemed anxious for a compromise. The West Indies, traditionally, has never been financially strong in its cricket. Realizing
this, its officials have rarely stood in the way of its players
earning as much money as they could in other parts of the
world. But when the vote to ban the players from Test matches
was taken on 26 July, the Windies voted with the strength.

EIGHT

Despite the furore around and about them, the Australians were still involved in a cricket tour. The Second Test, scheduled for the famous Old Trafford Ground at Manchester on 7 July, was looming and the tourists were busy working on the lessons of the First Test. Lurking in the minds of Chappell and his co-selectors Marsh and Walters was a nagging worry about the state of the Old Trafford pitch. Since before the Prudential Trophy game there on 2 June, the ground had been without a groundsman. The previous groundsman had left after a dispute with the Lancashire county club, and the TCCB's inspector of wickets, Mr Bert Lock, was supervising the preparation of the Test strip in a series of flying visits to the city. Apart from that, the pitch had been taking spin in most county games, with local off-spinner Jack Simmons claiming 6/8 in one spell and Derbyshire's Geoff Miller taking 6/54 in another game there.

Nevertheless, Chappell had reason to be fairly happy with the form of most of his players as the two days practice leading up to the Test began. The non-first-class fixture against Combined Universities at Oxford had been drawn, Nottinghamshire accounted for by an innings, and draws that favoured the tourists achieved against Derbyshire and Yorkshire. It was the form of his batsmen that was most pleasing in this two-week break between the Tests. Gary Cosier had hit 100 against Notts, Ian Davis seemed to have found the secret with 72 against Notts and 53 against Derby, the elegant Kim Hughes had put real pressure on the selectors with 95 at Nottingham and 92 against Derby, Craig Serjeant scored his first century under Australian colours with a scintillating 159 against Notts, and Richie Robinson had scores of 77, 54 and 33 not out leading up to the Test. In the Yorkshire game at Scarborough, Max Walker had given the tourists a big psychological boost when he had Geoff Boycott lbw for 0 to the third delivery of the innings. But the determined Boycott fought back with a second innings century, and celebrated in a way that was to become familiar to the tourists—bat and cap held high with both hands.

It was now public knowledge that Boycott had decided to end his self-imposed exile from Test cricket. On the Saturday before England's First Test side was announced, he had telephoned chairman of selectors Alec Bedser to say he now wished to be considered as available for England teams. Mr Bedser gave no guarantees, but the Packer saga had changed the outlook of many people. Boycott, for the first three years of his exile, had been the butt of trenchant—and in my view justified—criticism. Now, many who had pilloried him only months before, were clamouring for his selection. Some were even advocating that he take over the captaincy from Brearley after the Second Test. I was, and still am, of the opinion that it was unjust and unfair to young cricketers to recall Boycott. Whatever the reasons for his unavailability—and he has never made them known—I believed Boycott had deserted England when it needed him most. Was it merely coincidental that he now found himself physically and mentally adjusted to returning to an England team that was on the upturn in the wheel of fortune, after several seasons of humiliation at the hands of express bowlers from Australia and the West Indies? There was, and is, no doubting Boycott's ability. He is still an outstanding opening batsman in any side, in any language.

Still, the selectors felt they owed Dennis Amiss one more chance in Test cricket. Amiss, for all his failures against the pace men, had at least been there and fighting during Boycott's absence. Now, however, he knew his Test berth was on the line. Success for him at Manchester was vital, even if, as a late signatory with the Packer troupe, his future in Test cricket was in doubt. The England selectors, in fact, were impressed enough by the First Test draw to leave the 12 unchanged. Amiss and Graham Barlow came under close scrutiny but were given another chance, Amiss for obvious reasons and Barlow because the selectors were reluctant to write off such a fine athlete in the field without giving him every chance to prove himself. But the indications already were that Barlow would be 12th man, with Geoff Miller coming into the side for his first Test against Australia. England, like Australia, felt the need for two spinners in this game.

And behind the speculation about the turning wicket was the memory of 1956, when Jim Laker took 19 wickets for 90 on the Old Trafford dust-bowl. Australian manager Len Maddocks had every reason to remember that particular humiliation—he had been Laker's 9th and 19th victims of the match. The selectors reacted predictably when they named their Second Test team. Davis for Robinson was the only change in the 12, although it was now a foregone conclusion that the two spinners, O'Keeffe and Bright, would play. The one question remaining, then, was which of the pace bowlers would be landed with the drink-waiter's job. Pascoe, on the basis of his successful debut at Lord's, didn't deserve it: there was also a feeling within the Australian camp that Thomson might be a surprise choice. He had failed to impress senior team members by his late withdrawal from the county fixture against Yorkshire, just prior to the Test. That seemed an extreme, punitive measure however, and it was hardly likely that the Australians would go into a Test match without their acknowledged spearhead, especially as he had captured eight victims at Lord's.

Thus it was that on a fine and sunny 7 July morning, Greg Chappell won the toss and elected to bat on a wicket which was the subject of much speculation. It had been fanned that morning by the irrepressibly controversial Tony Greig, who had launched strong criticism at the Old Trafford pitch in particular, and English groundsmen in general. In his column in the mass-circulation London *Sun*, Greig said he could not understand why Test matches were still played at Old Trafford. 'So many wickets produced there are reported to the authorities as being unplayable', he said. And he added: 'It's about time the groundsmen started using less top-dressing and more elbow grease in their preparation of wickets—for more money of course'. Predictably, there was a furious reaction led by Lancashire chairman Cedric Rhoades, who called for disciplinary action against the ex-captain. Before the Second Test was an hour old, the Test and County Cricket Board announced that the article had been referred to its disciplinary sub-committee. Greig was reprimanded and his county, Sussex, fined £500 ($800). It was typical of the summer of '77. Hardly a ball was bowled without a backdrop of anger or argument.

On the field, both teams had plumbed for an extra bowler in their line-ups. Pascoe was the man who made way for Ray Bright's Test debut after five matches of experience as 12th man, while the Derbyshire off-spinner and batsman Geoff Miller came in at the expense of Barlow. Miller had played one previous Test—the fifth against the West Indies in 1976—and had toured India, Sri Lanka and Australia with the MCC side, being considered unlucky to miss out on a place in the Centenary Test team.

The Test was only 20 minutes and five overs old when Australia's perennial problem—lack of solidity in the openers —was again apparent. McCosker, whom I considered fortunate to have retained his place, was out for two when he failed to cover a lifting delivery from Willis and edged it to third slip, where Chris Old knocked the ball up and completed the catch. Willis had looked a threat from his first over when he tested McCosker with a dangerous bouncer which the Australian had been ill at ease in avoiding. The gangling fast bowler was extracting plenty of life from the pitch, far more than his fast bowling confederates, John Lever and Old.

Greg Chappell strode to the wicket at 1/4 in his usual role of attempting to rescue his side from a bad start. In the hot and sultry Manchester air, he proceeded to wrest the initiative from the England bowlers with a series of strokes that only he—and perhaps two or three others in the world—can manufacture. He got off the mark, glancing Willis finely for four, then was on the back-foot, clipping the same man past point for another boundary. Mike Brearley was as keen as any of us to discover what vagaries the pitch had; he introduced Underwood to the bowling crease after only 12 overs, and 24 runs. But it took only four overs for the realization that this wicket was no spinner's paradise—not yet anyway. Davis, whose dedication to the cause of grafting runs had shown a remarkable improvement, and Chappell had no trouble contending with the subtleties of the left-arm spinner. Chappell continued in glorious fashion, unleashing a succession of boundary shots—a square cut from Old, sweep from Underwood, then clipping Old off his legs. This last four gave him six boundaries in 37 runs as Australia recovered to 1/48. Davis' contribution had been only three singles in his first 80 minutes, but his occupation of the crease was an important contribution to his team. Brearley, sensing a Chappell takeover, introduced a fifth bowler—Greig—after only 20 overs, just after Davis had posted the Australian 50 in 80 minutes, sweeping Underwood for his first four. Now he felt confident enough to go on the attack, twice hitting Old off the back-foot speedily through the field, then lofting an Underwood no-ball high over mid-wicket. Chappell moved to 44 with a straight driven boundary from Greig and Australia at 1/80 seemed poised for a commanding day. Then Greig, as is his wont, struck an important blow. He moved a delivery fractionally away from the confident Australian captain whose thin edge was held by a delighted Alan Knott in front of Brearley at first slip. Chappell's 44 runs had come in 95 minutes with 7 fours and the packed Old Trafford house of 18,000 fans had seen a mini-jewel of an innings.

Straight after lunch, Davis slashed Willis inelegantly over slips but his grafting innings ended on 34 with the score at 96. Old got a ball to cut back prodigiously from the off, and a surprised Davis got an inside edge. The remarkable reflexes of Knott enabled him to recover from his initial movement to the right and hold a difficult chance low down to his left. The decline of the Australian middle-order was not about to abate. Craig Serjeant, after a confident start, reached only 14 before he was beaten and lbw to a Lever delivery which came back and hit high on the front pad with Australia 4/125. While Davis and Chappell had both appeared unhappy with the decisions that signalled their demise, Serjeant was quickly away from the crease, apparently satisfied with umpire Bill Alley's assessment of the situation. Hookes joined Walters, who had begun confidently for once, producing a glorious straight-drive off

The disease that afflicted the Australians throughout the series. Rick McCosker dives but cannot catch Tony Greig at Lord's, one of 17 chances the tourists missed.   Patrick Eagar photo.

Happier times. England captain Tony Greig is greeted by Australian Cricket Board treasurer Ray Steele (left) and chairman Bob Parish (centre) before the Centenary Test in Melbourne last March.   *Age* photo.

Sporting revolution-
aries. Kerry Packer
(left) chats with Ron
Barassi, the best known
and most successful
Australian football
coach in Melbourne,
last June. At right is
North Melbourne FC
president Lloyd
Holyoake.
Age photo.

'From now on, it's
every man for himself
and the devil take the
hindmost.' A dis-
appointed Kerry
Packer talks to
reporters after the
breakdown of his talks
with the ICC at Lord's
on 23 June.
UPI photo.

Irrational hitting was too often the cause of the Australian batsmen's downfall. Here, Rod Marsh swings hopefully at Geoff Miller during the Second Test to be caught at point.   Patrick Eagar photo.

Despite England's ascendancy, opening batsman Dennis Amiss still had uncomfortable moments like this, at the hands of Jeff Thomson. Amiss was dropped after the Second Test.   Patrick Eagar photo.

The much-improved Bob Willis—England's main striking force with 27 wickets in the series—bowling in the Second Test at Old Trafford.   Patrick Eagar photo.

Tony Greig, bitterly criticized by many for his part in the Packer affair, was still an important part of the England success. Here he drives O'Keeffe during his innings of 76 in the Second Test.   Patrick Eagar photo.

Greg Chappell hooks Bob Willis for 4, on the way to a splendid 112 in a lost cause in Australia's second innings of the Second Test, at Old Trafford. Patrick Eagar photo.

Alan Knott sweeps O'Keeffe
for four in the course of his
135 in the Third Test at Trent
Bridge, during a match-
winning stand of 215 with
Geoff Boycott.
Patrick Eagar photo.

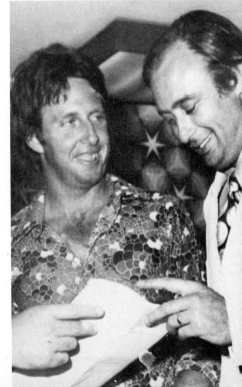

Australian fast bowler
Jeff Thomson and his agent,
David Lord. Mr Lord was
instrumental in Thomson's
breakaway from the Packer
troupe in July.

Greig after only a few minutes at the crease. But Hookes was unable to halt the slide, as he was 5th man out with only 140 runs on the board. The talented young left-hander's contribution was only 5 when he flashed at Lever, and Knott jubilantly threw his third catch of the innings into the air. Hookes was reluctant to accept the inevitable, but he had nothing to blame but his own rashness. The batsmen had thrown away, comprehensively, Chappell's tremendous advantage in winning the toss on a wicket that held none of the terrors predicted for it.

The enigmatic Walters, still without a century in 14 Tests in England, was in full flow, however. His lightning reflexes and inventiveness enabled him to handle Willis, Lever and Old with disdain and flying feet made sure that Underwood's spin was no threat. At last he found an ally—and who better than his incorrigible mate, Rod Marsh. The pair swung Australia around to a position of respectability in a sixth wicket stand of 98 sensible runs in 123 minutes.

Brearley kept ringing the bowling changes, but strangely would not risk the off-spin of Miller, who ostensibly was in this match for his bowling. Perhaps he felt the lad's inexperience would allow the hard-hitting Walters and Marsh to take command of the innings. As it was Miller bowled one over after tea, which cost only two runs, and was not called on until 35 minutes before stumps with the pair in full flight.

Walters, 47 at tea in a total of 5/162, reached his half-century after the break with a straight-driven four—his 8th—off Willis in 114 minutes. Marsh was sacrificing his normal game for studied defence, although occasionally he allowed himself some licence against Underwood. The 50 partnership came in only 47 minutes, then Marsh hit out at Old, bringing up the 200 in 280 minutes off 68.5 overs. At 5/226, Brearley relented and got an ironic cheer from the fervent England supporters when Miller marked out his run. Almost immediately, he had his first Australian wicket. Marsh, on 36, with Australia 5/238, lost patience and lashed optimistically at the third ball of Miller's fourth over. It flew from a thick edge high into the air and Amiss at point accepted the easiest of catches. The burly Marsh had earlier sent England fieldsman Bob Woolmer to hospital for an x-ray, after a vicious cut had struck him just above the right wrist. The injury certainly caused him no inconvenience the next day.

Walters had reached 81 on Marsh's departure and at last his supporters could see that elusive century. Despite his chain-smoking, nerveless exterior, the remarkable New South Welshman nursed a burning ambition to reach three figures in a Test match on English soil; the years of criticism about his technique on English wickets had been noted and Walters has made a habit of putting egg on critics' faces. His previous highest Test score in this country was 86, at Old Trafford in 1968, 22 innings earlier. That was passed as he notched his 15th boundary, putting Miller away wide of slip. But the magical 100 was not to be. Walters moved into a full-toss from Miller and the shot whistled thigh-high to Tony Greig at cover. Greig doesn't miss chances like that. A mightily unhappy Walters made his way to the pavilion amid sympathetic applause. His innings of 88 in 205 minutes had righted his team from an ugly tilt earlier in the day, and when stumps were drawn one run later, the total was 7/247 with Bright having made his first Test run and O'Keeffe still to score. Still, Brearley could afford to be well pleased with his team's effort in the field.

With Manchester's weather holding perfect, Bright and O'Keeffe held up the progress of the England bowlers for 51 minutes and 25 runs on the second morning. There was little hint of aggression, apart from one Bright sweep to the ropes, but it was a valuable rear-guard action for the tourists. It ended finally when O'Keeffe once again succumbed to the hook, Willis inducing a top-edge which Knott caught with ease. Bright, after 74 minutes of defiance, was caught in the slips for the same score, 12, before Max Walker and Thomson added a valuable 25 runs in 27 rollicking minutes when Walker swung at Underwood and missed. It was Underwood's first success in 20.2 overs that cost 53 runs. Australia, all out for 297, had not taken advantage of batting first, but it was a decided improvement on 5/140. Brearley had used six bowlers, all of whom had claimed a victim, the most successful being Lever, 3/60 off 25 overs.

At 2.32, twenty-two minutes after lunch, that total of 297

was looking gigantic to English eyes. By then, openers Brearley and Amiss were back in the pavilion with only 23 runs scored. The pair had survived 24 hair-raising minutes from Thomson and Walker before lunch while 12 runs were added. But their luck ran out after the resumption. Brearley was the first to succumb to Thomson's lively pace with the score 19. He played with the bat well away from the body and the edge flew low and hard to McCosker at second slip. That fieldsman could not grasp it cleanly but the alert Chappell, beside him, dived and held the ball before it reached the sanctuary of the grass. Amiss followed his captain in the next over from Walker, bowling from the Stretford end. The out-of-form opener aimed an ambitious hook at a delivery too far up to him. It flew from the top edge, clipped his shoulder and Chappell, stepping back a few paces from slip, held the skier.

Woolmer, the First Test century maker, was joined by Randall in a decidedly shaky English position. Woolmer, in fact, was lucky to survive his second ball from Thomson which flew untouched through the slips cordon to the boundary. The pair seemed to agree that attack was the solution to the problem. With a deal of luck, they took the game right away from Australia in an exhilarating third wicket stand of 142 in 162 minutes. Randall was looking for runs immediately, cutting Walker for four, then having a slice of fortune when a thick edge from Thomson narrowly avoided Craig Serjeant in the gully. Chappell wasted no time in calling on the services of Bright and O'Keeffe but he must have been bitterly disappointed with the result. Bright, in particular, refused to flight the ball, pushing it through at a speed reminiscent of Underwood, with something less than that man's fine skill. Randall found this a luxury to be consumed eagerly and took heavy toll with a series of sweeps and severe back foot shots in an arc from point to extra cover. O'Keeffe was lax in line and suffered a similar fate. Woolmer, blossoming in the confidence of his First Test triumph, was almost as impressive as his partner. The 50 partnership was posted in 59 minutes, the 100 exactly 50 minutes later. Although he would never admit it, Chappell must have already been regretting his decision to drop Pascoe. There was no help in the pitch for his slow men, although their form was so poor it is doubtful if they could have used it to advantage.

Australia's hopes of stopping the run-rampage were not helped by poor catching. Woolmer, on 43, presented McCosker at second slip with a straightforward chance off Thomson. But the gods were firmly set against the fieldsman. He appeared to attempt to throw the ball in the air but instead he had the mortification of seeing it on the ground. Woolmer was to give another, much more difficult chance on 59, when Walters, throwing himself to the right, could not hold onto a fierce drive. Walker was the bowler out of luck.

Randall raced to his half-century in 86 minutes, when he swept O'Keeffe for his ninth boundary. The Australians were growing frustrated and their outcricket began to show signs of amateurishness. Chappell's habit of throwing the ball back to Marsh whenever he fielded backfired when a careless return ballooned over the wicketkeeper's head for overthrows. It was not a good example for the captain to set and soon enough normally reliable fieldsman Hookes and Walters were making basic errors.

Woolmer, unaffected by the blow on his wrist the previous day, brought up his 50—his third in three innings of the series —in 133 minutes with 7 fours as he turned Thomson off his hip for three. Chappell refused the temptation to bowl either himself or Walters, who had been suffering from a minor shoulder injury which made bowling a painful experience. Instead, he relied on his four front-line men, Walker, Thomson, Bright and O'Keeffe. On this day, however, they let him down, giving scant heed to the tenets of line and length. It was not until 5.40 p.m. that the Australians broke through. Then Bright deceived Randall with a curving yorker that hit the batsman on the boot. Umpire Alley was in agreement with Bright's *sotto voce* appeal and Randall departed for 79, not before he and Marsh had indulged in a series of melodramatic gestures and lip movements. Randall's runs had been earned in 162 minutes with 12 fours and a five (from overthrows).

Woolmer was guiding England's destiny now, as he was joined by Greig, who had begun this Test with the news that 1978 wouldn't be his benefit year with Sussex after all. The

72

South African, who was awarded his county cap in 1967, had been anticipating his benefit, indeed planning had begun. A pop concert at Wembley involving Mick Jagger and the Rolling Stones, and possibly Neil Diamond, was on the drawing board. Instead, Sussex had awarded the benefit to Peter Graves, a batsman capped two years after Greig. Sussex secretary, Stanley Allen, in announcing the switch, said with face straight, 'It has nothing to do with the fact that Greig has joined the Packer Supertest team'. All the same, the heat was growing intense in Greig's kitchen and he was in the mood to take it out on the Australian bowlers. At first though he was content to help Woolmer hold on until stumps when England was 3/206, a fighting recovery from 2/23.

If the second day had been highlighted by an aggressive fightback by the home side, the third was devoid of anything memorable on the field. In six hours of fine weather, on a wicket described overnight by Randall as the best on which he had played, England laboured for 230 runs and the loss of six wickets. Tom Watson's British Open golf victory helped to compensate for a bored press contingent. Admittedly, by stumps, there were only two results possible—a draw or an England victory. But the policy of the batsmen throughout the day had been indeterminate against lacklustre bowling. Indeed, it was only the inertia of the batsmen that persuaded Thomson and Walker to return to their old habits of line and length, after lunch.

Thomson and Bright had taken up the attack when play started, but with neither Greig nor Woolmer in a risk-taking mood, Chappell soon gave himself six overs, for negligible result. He retired to give Walker and Thomson a chance with the new ball, taken at 3/225 after 86 overs. The patient Woolmer reached his century shortly after, off an uppish shot through the slips off Thomson who rewarded him with a look of utter anguish. He had been at the wicket for four and a half hours, with 15 fours. Greig was in no hurry, and seemed to delight in tormenting the bowlers, giving little hint of his normal aggression.

By lunch, the pair had carried on to 288, only nine runs short of the Australian total, and there were seven wickets still standing. Once again, the tourists had been slipshod in the field, Woolmer once collecting five runs from a defensive prod that yielded not one, but two separate overthrows. It wasn't until 45 minutes after lunch that Australia got the break it had needed so badly in the first half of the day. To make matters worse, three of the tourists were carrying injuries, the most serious being Marsh's strained right thigh, which restricted his mobility. O'Keeffe was having daily treatment to drain fluid off a joint in what is colloquially known as his spinning finger and Hookes was in pain from a bruised knee. It was something of a surprise to all concerned when Woolmer, after six hours and twenty minutes, pushed forward to O'Keeffe and gave short-leg Davis an easy catch. Woolmer's 137 had helped England to 4/325, 28 runs in front, and had created one of those obscure records that cricket fanatics around the world delight in unearthing. His century was his third in four innings against Australia on English soil—starting with his 149 in the second innings of the Fourth Test at The Oval in 1975. The previous best was three hundreds in five innings, by Maurice Leyland in 1934.

From this point, the England innings became nondescript, except for one giant act of aggression by Greig. A soaring straight drive off O'Keeffe headed straight for the elevated Manchester press box, set back 40 metres from the boundary rope; a magnificent blow designed, it seemed to the cynics, for those who had been tormenting Greig for nearly two months. The Australians by now were treating Greig with a certain amount of disrespect so sure were they that he had been out at 40 when a Thomson flier appeared to nudge the face of his bat on its way through to Marsh. But umpire Tom Spencer was without the benefit of the instant replay and the ebullient South African was allowed to continue. And continue he did until nearly 3.30 p.m. After a painstaking 244 minutes and 79 runs, he half-drove at Walker without being to the pitch and the big, awkward Victorian, carrying through with the momentum grabbed a magnificent left-handed catch only inches from the ground. England was now 5/348 and Greig had hit 11 boundaries and a six to still the tongues that were attempting to remove him from the team on the grounds of poor form.

Miller, in his first Test against Australia, struggled in-effectually for 40 minutes, especially against O'Keeffe, who made light of his handicap to bowl unchanged in the afternoon session. Five minutes before tea, Miller assayed a hook at Thomson and paid the penalty as the ball shot straight up and down into Marsh's gloves. At tea, England was 6/367, with Knott meandering on 30 and Old still to score. One hundred and fifteen minutes later, only another 69 runs had been added for the loss of three wickets, hardly the type of late-order batting that the situation demanded.

Brearley, in my mind, should have been aiming for quick runs and the chance to bowl two or three overs at Australia before stumps. The tourists, after almost two full days in the field in tiring heat, would have been at their most vulnerable. Instead, tailenders Derek Underwood and Willis were occupying the crease at the finish of play. Knott stayed 39 minutes after tea for 9 runs before he tried his famous slash over slips against Thomson. This time, however, O'Keeffe had been moved to almost a fly-slip and took a remarkable catch low down to make England 7/377. Old, with an occasional hint at aggression, and Lever, with none, took the score to 404, before Bright got a ball to turn sharply and jump, before flicking Lever's off stump. As a wicket, it was useful enough; as a sign of things to come, it must have made every Australian batsman wish he was elsewhere. The dreaded Old Trafford pitch had given its first hint of unpredictability, and Australia faced a long battle for survival. There was time for one more dismissal before stumps when Old, after 37 runs in 77 minutes, drove lustily at Walker. Bright, at second slip, juggled the ball before it finally settled in the gloved hands of Marsh. England, 9/436, held a lead of 139 with two days remaining after the rest day. The lead should have been 200.

The Australians must have had misgivings about their task as they spent the rest day on golf courses in and around Manchester. And those who were anticipating a new and exciting summer at home with Mr Packer, got the news that the man reputed to be the world's fastest bowler, West Indian Michael Holding, had come out of semi-retirement to sign for the Supertests.

If England's tactics of batting on and on, hoping for the wicket to wear enough to allow Underwood to weave his evil spell, had attracted criticism over this weekend, they were totally vindicated on the fourth day. Play began quietly enough, with only one run being added before Underwood, obviously anxious to begin bowling, aimed a swipe at Bright, missed and was bowled for 10 runs—in 53 minutes, mind you. England, all out for 437, led by 140. Bright, statistically, was the most successful bowler with 3/69 off 35.1 overs in his first Test. In truth, Thomson, 3/73 off 38, Walker 3/131 off a marathon 54 overs, and even O'Keeffe, 1/114 off 36 overs, had been more impressive during the 727 minutes of England's innings.

It didn't require a computer to know that Australia needed disciplined and dedicated batting to extricate themselves from this position. McCosker took only three deliveries to show he was not prepared to display any of these characteristics. Like a man obsessed with the knowledge that one blow in the middle of the bat would bring it all back, he aimed an inane hook at Willis' third ball of the innings. Underwood, trotting around from wide mid-on, threw the ball exultantly in the air as Australia slipped to 1/0. McCosker's four innings in this series had been 23, 1, 2 and 0 and there was nothing more certain, watching his departure, than his dismissal from the Third Test side. Chappell was once again at the crease to appease a poor start, and from the start of his innings was stroking the ball with authority. Davis looked momentarily confident as he drove Lever off his legs for four but was destined to commit batting suicide. Before he did, however, Chappell was serving notice that defence was not his idea of rescue. He took risks, cutting Lever just short of Old at slip, then hooked Willis high over the despairing head of Lever at fine leg for six. Davis decided if it was good enough for his captain, it was good enough for him. But it wasn't, and Lever running fast and hard to his left, covered many yards to take a well-judged catch. Australia 2/30, last man 12. Then came, by the standards of this innings, a stand. Chappell and his new partner, Serjeant, added 44 in 31 minutes, 30 of them to Chappell. Underwood was on after only 9 overs, and the Australian leader immediately tried to hit him out of the attack. A pulled two, then successive straight-driven fours, cost Underwood 10 runs in three deliveries of his third over, and for a moment, it appeared that the genius of Chappell could turn the fortunes of his team.

The shrewd Underwood, however, lowered his trajectory a couple of degrees and concentrated on containment. Serjeant brought up the 50, off-driving Old to the ropes but he hardly looked confident. There was little surprise in either camp when Underwood forced him on the defensive, and the indecisive prod was snapped up by Woolmer at short-leg. Walters' arrival was greeted by the now-compulsory two gullies for the fast bowlers and Underwood had three men crowded around the bat as he wheeled down over after over from the Stretford end. Chappell reached his half-century, pulling Old through mid-wicket for his eighth boundary, in 90 minutes. Even though it was brilliant artistry, there was a hint of desperation to his innings, brought about by the abject lack of application displayed by his fellows. Walters was just the fourth example; with his captain wanting only solid defence to offset his dash, Walters was surprised by a delivery from Greig, brought on for the last over before lunch. It kept low and the raucous appeal was obviously to the liking of Umpire Spencer. So Australia at lunch was 4/92 and effectively giving away a one-nil lead in the Ashes series.

For 90 minutes after lunch, there came a serious attempt at consolidation. Chappell at last looked as if he had found an ally in David Hookes as the pair added 54 runs in 80 minutes. Hookes indeed outscored his more illustrious partner in this stanza, reaching 28 with a series of good shots and firm defence. But it couldn't last. The young left-hander became over-anxious in attempting to drive Miller, who once again had been called on belatedly. Hookes' feet were far from the pitch, the ball took the outside edge and flew gently to an elated Brearley at slip. A desperate situation, 5/146 called for stern application from Rodney Marsh. Instead, Chappell watched in horror as his vice-captain capitulated irresponsibly after troubling the attack for one run. Marsh, the hero of many Australian recoveries of yesteryear, aimed what can only be called an appalling cross-bat swish at Underwood, which travelled swiftly to Randall at mid-on. Even then, Marsh nearly got away with his indiscretion. Randall, that most spectacular of fieldsman, juggled the ball several times before finally holding on to it as he lay flat on his back. While Marsh trudged off, his feelings masked by the walrus-vastness of his moustache, Randall lay ashen-faced and motionless in mock horror on the Old Trafford turf.

Three balls later, Bright half-drove at Underwood and the bowler made no mistake with a sharp low chance. Australia was now 7/147, losing its last 3 wickets for one run in 23 deliveries. Now, even Chappell was in danger of running out of partners before his well-deserved century was reached. Enter then, Kerry O'Keeffe to play the role that had been required, but not forthcoming, from the start of the innings. He defended resolutely, refusing to take even the slightest risk, while Chappell went about the task of scoring runs. By tea, Chappell had advanced the score to 171, a lead of 31. He was then 92. Immediately afterwards, he hooked a Willis no-ball for 4, cover drove him for 2, and reached his 14th Test century with a classical straight drive for 4 off the same bowler. His innings had so far lasted 245 minutes, with 15 fours and a six and he was accorded a standing ovation by the big crowd, who quite rightly acknowledged that they would be waiting a long time before they saw one as good. The Chappell-O'Keeffe defiance lasted until 5.32 p.m. when the total was 202, 55 runs having been added in 95 minutes. When the great man was on 112, he stepped back to give himself room to cut Underwood and was bowled off the bottom edge by one that spun back sharply and kept low. Chappell's time at the crease had been 281 minutes in this his sixth three-figure score against England. Only Sir Donald Bradman (19), Arthur Morris (8) and Bill Lawry (7) have scored more, although Neil Harvey, Bill Woodfull and Victor Trumper achieved as many.

At 8/202, with nary a cloud in the sky, the Second Test was as good as lost or won, depending on your affiliations. Walker and Thomson made only token gestures with the bat, Walker falling to an excellent one-handed diving effort by Greig at silly point and Thomson skying a big hit to Randall at mid-on. Both victims went to Underwood who finished with 6/66 off 32.5

78

overs, 13 maidens. Underwood owed his success, not to a dusty, turning pitch but to his own adaptability. Only with the prized scalp of Chappell could he attribute help from the pitch. For the rest, he had varied his flight and his attack cleverly, especially as Brearley must have been toying with the idea of relieving him early in Chappell's rampage. So Australia was all out for 218 and England needed 79 to win in a day and 10 minutes.

Only O'Keeffe, 24 not out in a minute over the two hours had provided the support needed by Chappell to save, or even to have a slight chance of winning this Test match. On the second day, the normally taciturn Chappell had taken his team to task with a verbal blast at their lackadaisical attitude in the field. What he told them then was that they did not deserve the privilege of playing for Australia. What he was entitled to say to his batsmen now was that they were not entitled to the privilege of playing in the same team as he. It had been a display of totally careless, spineless batting, accentuated by the gross transgressions that accounted for the dismissals of McCosker, Davis, Serjeant, Hookes, Marsh and Bright. Only Walters had any sort of excuse, lbw to a delivery that conceivably was too high and too wide of the leg-stump.

England, 0/8 when the last day began, was in some trepidation about the mounting rain clouds that packed around the famous old ground when play began. But the fates acknowledged that Australia did not deserve such a reprieve. It was 12.34 when Dennis Amiss, in his 50th and perhaps last Test, produced the winning cover drive off O'Keeffe. England lost only one wicket in scoring its victory, that of Brearley after a 75-run opening stand. The captain, only minutes from learning that he had been appointed as leader of his country for the rest of the series, had made 44 when he drove O'Keeffe gently to Walters at cover. Woolmer was in only long enough for Amiss to take his personal tally to 28 not out as he completed the nine-wicket triumph, England's first home victory in 14 Test matches stretching back to the Indian series of 1974. It was also the home country's second success in 14 Tests against Australia, and the 8th in 41 encounters since World War II.

Chappell lost no time in making his feelings public. At a

press conference immediately following the game, he said he was looking strongly at the possibility of opening in the Third Test himself, as well he might after starts of 25, 5, 2 and 0 in the series. The tactic of sending only two recognized openers on the arduous five-month tour had not endeared Messrs Ridings, Harvey and Loxton to Chappell. Indeed, chairman of selectors Phil Ridings who watched the Test from the viewpoint of a holidaymaker could have been excused for asking himself the reason for sending several of the players on this the most sought-after of all cricket experiences.

Chappell added that he was particularly disturbed about the poor fielding and the lack of fight shown by some players. He could have added, in particular, that the example of vice-captain Marsh was not all he would have wished. 'It is alright saying the side is inexperienced, but that is no excuse—we have no excuses', was his summing up.

I wrote in the Melbourne *Age*, after this loss, that there had been a complete disintegration in the spirit of the team. There was- and is-no doubt in my mind that the Packer affair and all its ramifications had undermined the confidence of many players who, with all their worries, had lost the singlemindedness to apply themselves to the job of winning or at least fighting and using all their undoubted talent to the end. There were four Packer players in the England side, Greig, Knott, Underwood and Amiss, and with the exception of Amiss, they were playing the game as if their reputations depended on it. Most of the Australians were of the opinion that the world was against them and were playing accordingly.

Chappell was determined that his charges were going to work damn hard to redeem themselves when the Third Test began at Trent Bridge on 28 July. The itinerary allowed for a couple of days off, and his party split up all over the country. Before they left, however, they were ordered to be in Northampton on the following Friday for compulsory net practice, the first time the entire squad of 17 had been assembled for a county game, and the first net practice ordered before a county game since the opening of the tour against Surrey on 30 April. Chappell himself was off to the tennis courts to challenge Doug Walters whose reputation had grown since he had partnered former Australian champion Mark Edmondson to victory in a pro-am invitation event during the Wimbledon fortnight in June.

While Australia was faced with the task of fighting back to the ascendancy it had enjoyed in recent years, England was in the comfortable position of looking to see how best it might strengthen its already strong combination. Opening batsman Dennis Amiss was the man most likely to be dropped in view of his innings of 4, 0, 11 and 28 not out. There was a man breathing heavily on his neck—one Geoffrey Boycott who, even as Amiss hit the winning runs at Old Trafford, was making another century for Yorkshire, this time at Trent Bridge against Nottinghamshire. The word was that the England selectors had brought themselves to a decision to forgive and forget. Boycott, it appeared, would be recalled. Amiss had not done enough to keep him out.

NINE

There were no rest days for the commanders of the two combatants now facing up to the fiercest battle in the long history of calm and conservative cricket. The Test and County Cricket Board met at Lord's on 15 July to formulate the policy England would follow at the ICC meeting 11 days later. Each of the 17 counties was represented under the chairmanship of former Essex and England batsman Doug Insole. It was a short session—less than two hours—and no statement was made at its conclusion. But the TCCB had decided to press for Test bans on the Packer players. As well, a majority of counties had voted in favour of banning the same players from county cricket from season 1978, a decision it planned to make public at its next meeting on 5 August. The Board delegates also discussed sanctions against counties who insisted on playing cricketers already signed with the rebel troupe. Cricket authorities, it seemed, were preparing the most ruthless punishment possible for those who had fallen for the lure of the television dollars.

The Establishment could afford one smile of relief on 18 July when England's most colourful umpire H. D. 'Dicky' Bird announced that he had turned down the offer of a three-year contract to join the Packer organization. Bird, a 44-year-old bachelor who played county cricket for Yorkshire and Leicestershire before turning to umpiring, said: 'I've always been a loyalist and always will be. It was a very good offer, well above anything I get over here, but I knew I could give only one answer.' Ten days later, Bird was scheduled to stand in his 12th Test match, and on the same day, two Australian umpires Max O'Connell and Lou Rowan declined offers to join the rebels.

O'Connell, one of the country's best, had stood in the Centenary Test and Rowan, a detective in the Queensland police force, retired several years ago after a distinguished umpiring career.

The Packer organization was going ahead with its plans to set up the controversial Supertest series; there would be no turning back. In a greenhouse just outside the gates of VFL Park, Melbourne, curator John Maley and his workers were about to launch one of the most remarkable experiments in the game's history: the building of artificial cricket pitches away from the grounds on which they were to be used. Mr Packer and his rebels knew they were facing an uphill battle to gain permission to use established cricket grounds for the Supertests and other games. The trusts that administer the Melbourne and Brisbane cricket grounds and the authorities that control the Adelaide Oval and the Perth ground work hand-in-hand with the respective State associations, and their attitude to the troupe was widely known. Sydney was to be another story.

Mr Packer had claimed from the start of the controversy that he had arranged alternative grounds in each city. The biggest problem was to provide pitches of an acceptable standard for the class of cricket that was to be played. The answer began to emerge in the greenhouse adjacent to VFL Park where eight massive concrete tubs were installed. Four of the tubs, each 3.25 centimetres thick, would be used as a cradle for the pitch. Maley was preparing two pitches for the Melbourne venue, each 12.2 metres long, 3 metres wide and 31 centimetres deep. After a base of gravel, sand and loam was laid in the tubs, Maley and his team began the revolutionary task of making the pitches from Merri Creek soil, the basic ingredient of Melbourne Cricket Ground pitches for many years. After hours, days, weeks of rolling, tamping and levelling the soil, grass seedlings were sown and nurtured under 80 arc lamps which created a constant temperature of 75 degrees Fahrenheit. By mid-September, a thick bed of grass covered both strips and Maley was able to mow it for the first time. Transferring the pitches from their artificial beds to the centre of the ground was another problem for which an ingenious answer appeared to have been found. To allay fears that cranes carrying the concrete tubs would damage the ground, Packer's brains trust came up with the idea of using the hovercraft principle to move the tubs. This would involve the building of a skirting around the tubs. In the words of Maley: 'Then we force air underneath them, create a vacuum and haul them through the front of the glasshouse and into the stadium'. In the middle, the concrete trays and the pitch would be slipped into the 55.8 centimetre deep trench dug for it. This was scheduled to take place in mid-October, in time for the grass and the surrounding soil to blend together before the first Supertest in Melbourne on 2 December. Maley believed this system of preparation would provide the best pitches possible in the time available.

'They will be far better than they would have been had they been prepared in a conventional way', he said. His only fear was the short journey from greenhouse to stadium. 'I shudder to think what would happen if they dropped', he admitted. A similar scheme was underway to prepare pitches for Football Park, in Adelaide, venue for the Packer games in that city.

Maley was fully aware of the important role he was playing. For despite the legal battles, the bans, and general ill-feeling now rampant in cricket circles, the success or failure of the whole Packer plan depended very much on the standard of pitches used for the troupe's matches. If the world's best bowlers were able to wreak havoc on substandard wickets, the viewing public would quickly lose interest. With fast bowlers of the calibre of Michael Holding, Wayne Daniel, Dennis Lillee, Andy Roberts, John Snow and Mike Procter bowling at venomous pace, even the world's best batsmen needed reliable wickets to make the matches legitimate contests.

There was another, minor problem at VFL Park. Because of the unusually wet Melbourne winter, the centre area of the ground was virtually bereft of grass. This meant artificial turf would have to be used for the bowlers' run-ups, another first for cricket in Australia. All the same, Packer authorities in Australia were happy enough with the practical progress being made towards the staging of the matches.

In other areas, however, the battle between the conventional game and the rebels raged unabated. On 22 July, the five Pakistanis involved with Packer declared themselves unavailable for the series against England in Pakistan in December and January. Asif Iqbal, acting as spokesman for his countrymen Imran Khan, Mushtaq Mohammed, Majid Khan and Zaheer Abbas, reiterated that the players were looking forward to participating in the Supertest series. Only a week before, the new Army-controlled government of Pakistan had told its Cricket Board of Control not to allow the five to take part in the rebel organization. How it planned to achieve this was not made clear. A few days earlier, Mushtaq had told me that he felt any ICC ban on the Packer players would be ineffective. Mushtaq, the current Pakistan captain, was leading Northamptonshire in its game against the touring Australians and like everyone else was convinced the ICC would slap a blanket Test ban on the 51 cricketers now believed to have signed with the promoting company J. P. Sport.

'I can't see such a ban working', Mushtaq said. 'I think when the countries need their top players for Test cricket, they will relax the ban.' Like all his fellow rebels, Mushtaq expressed the hope that there would be a compromise before the television series began. And he echoed the sentiments of many senior cricketers when he said he did not agree with the principle of a 'pirate' series in complete opposition to established cricket.

'But the administrators have had 100 years to improve pay and conditions for the players and they haven't made any progress', Mushtaq added. 'That is why I signed the contract without any hesitation—the administrators needed to be shocked into doing something for the majority of players.'

Mushtaq, 33, joined Tony Greig in his assertion that the troupe would be helping cricket in general by its actions. 'There will be at least 51 players in Australia in the summer. Those of us not engaged in games will be conducting coaching sessions at schools and clubs . . . For many years, players have not got just rewards for the huge money they have attracted through the turnstiles. Everyone agreed that it was a very poor situation, everyone except the administrators. Now something has been done about it, and somehow everyone seems upset.'

That, in a few short sentences, summed up the attitude of most of the experienced players who had signed with Packer. I agree that there were many grounds for resentment and for the climate that allowed so many players to sign up so readily. The main argument was whether they had chosen the right path to exemplify their feelings of defiance.

The 13 Australians in the touring party who were part of the rebel movement were not standing by saying nothing, either. On 22 July, Chappell called a team meeting at Leicester, the night before the tourists were to play Leicestershire, in the last game leading up to the Third Test at Trent Bridge. Chappell's main aim was to deliver yet another blast at his team for their slovenly fielding and lack of batting application which had not improved in the two county games since the Second Test. The meeting, however, developed into much more than a captain's harangue. During the game against Northamptonshire four days before, the normally reticent Chappell had felt obliged to issue his first—and only—verbal blast to an individual. It was directed at batsman Ian Davis for failing to chase a shot in the field. Now he spoke his mind to the team in general behind closed doors at the team's Leicester hotel. Then he threw the meeting open to each player in the 17 man party: 'If you feel you have anything worth saying, say it', implored the captain. There is no tape-recording or short-hand note of the meeting. But from what many of the team said later, plenty was said. Much of it was harsh; there was hardly a player who didn't receive his share of criticism. For a young team, one down in a series and on the receiving end of many insults, it was probably a mind-boggling but necessary occasion . . . if it was kept private. It wasn't.

One day later, on 23 July, a statement purporting to come from Chappell was issued in Sydney by J.P. Sport Pty Ltd, the promoter, in name, of the Packer series. The statement denied that there was any split in the Australian side over players' decisions. There were further statements that day from Sydney from the England players Tony Greig, Derek Underwood and Dennis Amiss refuting rumours that they had had second thoughts about their decisions to join the group.

According to Chappell's statement, several players had said at the team meeting that they were unhappy about reports that the team had split into two groups, those who had signed with Packer and those who had not. In the statement, Chappell said:

86

'I have done this with the view of not only clarifying our situation, but so the air can be cleared once and for all and we can get on with the job of retaining the Ashes in England'. A day later he was to tell reporters in England: 'the statement was made in the best interests of the team'.

The truth is that the statement was not the idea of Greg Chappell, or any of the players at the team meeting. I had been one of those writing reports that there was a split in feelings in the team. That came from a series of conversations, drinks, meals and social intercourse with several of the tourists. Further, while the team was staying in Birmingham for the match against Warwickshire, immediately prior to the Leicestershire engagement, Chappell had had a series of telephone calls from Packer representatives in Australia. These telephone calls influenced Chappell and the others to make a statement. So before the team ventured to Leicestershire, and before any team meeting, the captain's 'clarification' was at least in the formative stages.

On a technical point, the statement was instantly regarded by Australian authorities as illegal. This was because Greg Chappell had sought permission from team manager Len Maddocks to make it—and been refused. Maddocks regarded it as a breach of the Australian Cricket Board's tour contract conditions. He took the line that the contracts, signed by every player before the tour started, had been breached enough. Instead, he offered to issue a statement of his own, which said: 'I understand there have been rumours spreading to the effect that there is unrest in the Australian team, mainly due to the fact that some players are signed to play with the Kerry Packer organization, while others are not. The players unanimously have asked that I issue a statement to the effect that this is not the case. They have pride in their performances individually and collectively. They are performing to the best of their ability for Australia, will continue to do so, and are touring happily together.'

If Mr Maddocks hoped his statement would forestall any release from Sydney, from Chappell, he was wrong. And Australian Cricket Board officials were furious. To them, it seemed the tourists had been flouting their tour contracts blatantly. An example occurred in Manchester a few weeks before when a band of Packer rebels had made a rendezvous for the purpose of filming an advertisement for the Channel 9 network, under the direction of Channel 9 producer, John Crilly. This was in direct opposition to the tour contract, which stipulated that players could undertake no publicity or advertising without permission of officials. And tour manager Len Maddocks had no knowledge of that little outing.

Worse still, the Leicestershire team meeting resulted in a totally misleading front page story in a mass circulation paper, the *Daily Express*. The story alleged that the genial Victorian fast bowler Max Walker had threatened Maddocks with physical violence. The report charged that Walker had made his threat after a confrontation between Maddocks, Chappell and Rod Marsh 'at their Birmingham hotel on Friday night'. The fact that the Australians—all of them—were in Leicester, not Birmingham, on the Friday night, was overlooked. There were many harsh words spoken in Leicester that night; many of them unkind, most of them painfully true. If any threats were uttered against the manager, however, they certainly didn't come from the mouth of Walker.

Maddocks, a man not noted for making many official statements, was quite correct to issue one after that report. With the strength of righteous indignation behind him, he said: 'I don't usually comment on newspaper reports, but this one is so scurrilous the record has to be put straight. There was no threat of physical treatment made to me or by me or by anyone. A lot of words were spoken during the team meeting on Friday and at one time or another, some people were offended. This was the whole point of the meeting and everybody felt it did some good.'

Walker, by general acclaim as good-natured a cricketer as has ever represented his country, was upset enough to seek legal advice about the *Daily Express* story, but he did not take any action.

Like everyone else in the touring party, Maddocks had come in for his share of criticism at the meeting. It wasn't the first time. At Canterbury, during the second first-class fixture of the tour, vice-captain Marsh had chaired a team meeting in which

Mr Maddocks was asked to give his players earlier, and clearer, notice of the many obligations a touring side has to fulfil. In the early days, players were often left in the dark about the time and the style of dress for official functions. Still, it must be remembered that Mr Maddocks and his assistant, Brisbane taxation official Norm McMahon, were saddled with undoubtedly the most unenviable administrative job of any touring teams to England. As the representatives of the Australian Cricket Board, at least 13 of the 17 players had cause to regard Maddocks and McMahon hostilely so the pair was faced with the task of walking a tightrope of diplomacy and tact in running a successful team and avoiding a confrontation between 13 players who had committed themselves to a different organization. That they didn't succeed, in many ways is no reflection on their own particular good qualities as administrators.

On 23 July came the first indication that the cricket split could end in legal action. Mr Packer, in an interview in the Sydney *Sun-Herald*, stated that he would go the courts against the ICC if it banned any player. 'If this happens, we will claim restraint of trade', he said. He reiterated that he had secured enough grounds in Australia to stage a series of three matches between his Australian and West Indian sides, and three more between the Australians and a team drawn from the Rest of the World. He also estimated his investment in the venture now amounted to $4 million. Mr Packer revealed that he had offered the Australian Cricket Board $500,000 a year for five years for exclusive television rights: 'They talk about not being able to pay the cricketers enough. They could have had my money to do it.' And he repeated the assertion that if he had been given the television rights, he would not have started planning of the Supertests.

It is that statement that has always seemed to me to be the largest weakness in the case for the cricket rebellion. How can Mr Packer justify his interest in cricketers and their welfare while admitting the troupe would not have come into existence under his banner if he had been awarded what amounted to a lucrative bonus for his commercial television network?

Nonetheless, the practicalities of war could not be ignored.

On the same day, sporting editor of the Melbourne paper, *Sunday Press*, Ian McDonald, revealed exclusively the dates of the proposed Supertests, a week before they were due to be released by the Packer organization. McDonald's article showed that there would be direct clashes between four of the Supertests and the scheduled official Test matches between Australia and India. The Packer itinerary stated that the first three Supertests would be between Australia and the West Indies—by now, Mr Packer was claiming he had signed the entire West Indies Test squad—and the last three between Australia and the Rest of the World.

The first Supertest, in Melbourne from 2–6 December, clashed with the First Test in Brisbane from 2–7 December. The second Supertest, in Sydney from 16–20 December, clashed with the Second Test in Perth from 16–21 December. The third Supertest coincided with the Third Test, the Packer players competing in Adelaide from 31 December to 4 January while the official Test was in Melbourne from 30 December to 4 January. The fourth Supertest did not clash, being in Melbourne from 13–17 January while the Fourth Test was in Sydney from 7–12 January. The fifth Supertest in Perth from 27–31 January was in conflict with the last Test against the Indians, in Adelaide from 28 January–2 February. The sixth and last Supertest was scheduled for Sydney from 9–13 February.

The last Packer game would take place after the Australian touring side to the West Indies had departed, which made rather a mess of his claim that his players would be available for the tour if needed. Assuming the Packer men filled the bulk of the touring side—which they would if talent was the only deciding factor—how did he imagine eleven players would be found for the first game of the Caribbean tour? No one in the Packer organization would confirm the dates in the *Sunday Press* story of 23 July. When they became official, however, it appeared McDonald had made only one small error.

In fact, the Packer media empire was not having the best of luck with its releases of details of the great cricket revolution. The original story was to have been released in the *Bulletin* on the day before the Jubilee Test, 15 June. Instead, it was broken on 9 May. The dates of the Supertest were to be released on 1 August. Their premature publication brought only this reaction from Brian Treasure, the administrative controller of the company World Series Cricket, formed to deal with the running of the troupe activities: 'Naturally with only a limited number of weekends and long weekends available, there will be a clash of some dates with Test matches. But in deference to the cricketing public, World Cricket has planned its Supertest series itinerary so that no two Tests will be played in the same State at the same time.'

In September, the same Mr Treasure was to become angry when Melbourne *Age* cricket writer Mike Sheahan approached him for details of a Packer troupe game which involved the playing of a team of bowlers against a team of batsmen. There, at least, was one area in which the Packer people did not differ from most sporting organizations. They disliked sporting writers who wrote stories without their permission.

The release of the Packer playing dates was not exactly calculated to create a good impression with the ICC delegates, due to meet at Lord's only three days later. Concrete evidence that Mr Packer was planning to meet established cricket head-on in the Australian summer was hardly conducive to an atmosphere of compromise.

The news that reached Mr Packer from the chairman of the Sydney Cricket Ground Trust, Mr Pat Hills, on 25 July could hardly have been a surprise. Mr Hills said the Trust's long-term commitments to the New South Wales Cricket Association prevented it from granting permission for use of the ground to the Packer group. That meant the use of the five established first-class grounds in the five main cricket centres had been denied. Still, three weeks later, Mr Packer was able to announce that he had secured two football grounds (Melbourne and Adelaide), a trotting track (Perth) and an agricultural showground (Sydney) as the venues for his controversial venture. There was some speculation that he retained a slim chance of success in Sydney when, on 27 July the New South Wales Government sacked the 13-man SCG Trust. According to Mr Hills, the new Trust which was to be appointed by the Government, might look differently on the

91

Packer request. The Sydney television chieftain had reacted with some emotion to the news of his rejection by the SCG Trust, claiming the decision was made by a 'group of crusty old men sitting behind closed doors'.

'The SCG is the best ground and the people of Sydney have paid a great deal of money towards its creation and upkeep', he said. 'It's a pity they will not be given an opportunity to see the best cricketers play on the best ground, or be allowed to make the decision on whether the Test should be played there.' In the overall battle, however, that was one skirmish the rebels expected to lose.

In London, the forces of the Establishment, in this case the ICC, the parliament of world cricket, were massing for their meeting on 26 and 27 July. There was no disagreement that this was the ICC's most important gathering. The challenge had been thrown out and the highest court in the game had to decide how best to answer it.

There was no lack of politicking as the delegates from the six full and foundation member countries—England, Australia, West Indies, New Zealand, Pakistan and India—arrived in London. In addition, South Africa, currently under suspension because of its apartheid policies in sport, had made it clear it would abide by any ICC declarations. India and New Zealand, although none of their players was involved, were strongly on the side of banning the Packer players from Tests. After all, India would be in Australia and the England side in New Zealand during the southern summer of 1977-78 and both those countries would suffer if the Supertests went ahead. The West Indies was the only country likely to dissociate itself from a ban of Test players. Gentle pressure, including some words of warning about the 1978 Australian tour to the West Indies, had been whispered, however, and before the meeting began, West Indies Board chairman Jeff Stollmeyer was saying publicly that his country would be voting with the majority.

Mr Packer struck one more blow before the ICC met to make its inevitable decision. Speaking on television in Sydney, he declared that the cricketers who had signed up for the Supertest series could not back out of their contracts. He indicated that none of the players—whom he now numbered at

92

51—had indicated that they wanted to withdraw. Even if they wanted to, they couldn't, he said.

Mr Packer added that he was confident the Supertests would be a commercial success for the Channel 9 network. He was bolstered in that belief by a statement made the day before by Mr Sam Chisholm, general manager of his network. Chisholm said that Channel 9's direct telecast of the series between Australia and England had been an unqualified success. 'We have given Australia what no other station has been able to, and that is uninterrupted coverage of the series. For the first time since television came to Australia, we are giving audiences six or seven hours of Test coverage and the surveys show this is exactly what they want', he said.

It was ironic. A television executive giving facts and figures about the ratings battle only hours before the International Cricket Conference decided to ban the best cricketers in the world for being involved in that same ratings battle.

The men who congregated at Lord's on the morning of 26 July, one of most momentous days in a momentous year were, England: W. H. Webster (chairman), Freddie Brown, Doug Insole; Australia: Tim Caldwell, former ACB chairman, John Warr, Australia's England-based ICC representative; West Indies: Jeff Stollmeyer and Alan Rae; India: R. P. Mehra, Board of Control chairman and Ghulam Ahmed, Board secretary; Pakistan: Zafir Ahmed, Board of Control secretary; New Zealand: Walter Hadlee, a former Test captain, and Colin Cowdrey, New Zealand's England based representative.

It wasn't until 6.30 that evening that ICC secretary Jack Bailey emerged to give the attendant journalists the verdict, which was straightforward and rather more ruthless than most experts anticipated. The ICC had given the Packer rebels until 1 October to make up their minds. If they still wanted to play with the rebel troupe, they would be banned from Test cricket. The only way back was by express permission of the ICC, on application from individual countries. Mr Bailey was quick to point out that such permission would be extremely difficult to obtain. In addition, the ICC had urged each of its members to take similar action on a domestic level against the signed players. None of the Packer games would receive first-class status, none would be included in official records. Since the vote had been unanimous, the English county cricket competition, the Sheffield Shield in Australia, and the Shell Shield in the West Indies could expect to be without many of their respective stars from here on. About the only recognized part of cricket not to be disturbed was the current England-Australia series.

The ICC statement, read in full by Mr Bailey to a hushed audience, was:

At the meeting today, member countries gave long and earnest consideration to the effect of the Packer proposals on cricket at all levels and in all countries. They reaffirm the views of the Test-match playing countries, at their meeting on 14 June, that the whole structure of cricket, for which their governing bodies are responsible, could be severely damaged by the type of promotion proposed by Mr Packer and his associates.

Following the breakdown of negotiations with Mr Packer, when the Conference was unable to accede to his demand to exclusive TV rights in Australia, members of the ICC today unanimously resolved to ensure that it could honour its responsibilities to players at all levels. To do so, they are determined to continue to promote international matches between countries and to oppose to the maximum extent the series of exhibition matches arranged to take place in Australia during the forthcoming Australian summer. These matches will not rate as first-class, nor appear in official records. In order to give effect to these views the ICC passed unanimously a change in the ICC rules, relating to qualifications for Test matches: 'Notwithstanding anything herein before contained, no player who, after 1 October 1977, has played or has made himself available to play in a match previously disapproved by the Conference, shall thereafter be eligible to play in any Test match, without the express consent of the Conference, to be given only on the application of the governing body for cricket of the country for which, but for this sub-rule, the player would be eligible to play.'

In addition to this new rule, the Conference passed unanimously a resolution disapproving certain matches. This read: 'It is hereby resolved that any match arranged, or to be arranged by J. P. Sport Pty Ltd, Mr Kerry Packer, Mr Richie Benaud or associated companies or persons, to take place in Australia or elsewhere between 1 October 1977 and 31 March 1979 is disapproved.'

The Conference also passed a guidance resolution as follows: 'For future guidance, the Conference records and minutes that matches are liable to be disapproved if so arranged, whether by reference to date or otherwise, as to have the probable result that invitations to play in such matches will conflict with invitations which have been or may be received, to play in first-class matches subject to the jurisdiction of the governing bodies of foundation and full members of the Conference.

The Conference strongly recommended that each member country should pursue as soon as possible, at first-class level and in other domestic cricket activities, the implementation of decisions made in regard to Test matches.

The ICC reaction had been widely anticipated, yet I feel the news of the decision sent a huge shock wave through the world of cricket. Perhaps many of us had been hoping that the spectre of Mr Packer would somehow disappear, leaving the game intact, yet much the wiser for a fleeting intrusion. Now the cold, hard facts were being spelt out. Unless there was mass insurrection among the rebels, the names Greig, Underwood, Knott, Chappell, Marsh, Lillee, Thomson, Lloyd, Viv. Richards, Holding, Roberts, Mushtaq and Asif would never grace a Test match again.

The reaction from the banned players was one of resignation; they had expected the Test match ban, although some expressed surprise at the clear hint given to implement punitive measures at domestic levels.

Alan Knott: 'I am under contract to play for Kerry Packer and there is no way I'll change my mind about that. I am looking forward to a wonderful winter's cricket in Australia later this year.'

Derek Underwood: 'I am very sorry at the news because it could mean the end of my Test career. I have given the matter plenty of thought and I shall be sticking to my decision to play in the Packer series.'

John Snow: 'I am not the slightest bit surprised. None of us are.

95

When we went into this, we knew exactly what we were doing and that it would probably get us banned from Test and county cricket.'

Barry Richards: 'This is a big blow to the future of Test cricket. It is going to go back to being a real amateur game. The costs will be the same, but the receipts will be much less because they will have second teams out there.'

Asif Iqbal: 'For years, Test cricketers have not been paid what they deserve. Now suddenly England and Pakistan say they will pay their players more next season. So some good has come out of this business.'

Mike Procter: 'What have I done wrong? I don't see how they can suspend me for I'm not harming my South African national side. We have been out of Test cricket for seven years.'

Tony Greig: 'I'm not saying anything; no comment. I'm keeping quiet about this.'

Zaheer Abbas: 'When I signed for Packer, I knew my Test career with Pakistan was in jeopardy. I never dreamed I would risk losing my job with Gloucestershire.'

Predictable reactions. With hindsight, it would seem only Tony Greig had an inkling of what the next step would be. Up in Nottingham, the Australian reactions were very much the same, although at the time unprintable because, suddenly, contractual obligations were looming large in the minds of the tourists.

A particularly saddening aspect of the ICC statement was the mention, with its disparaging innuendo, of the former Australian captain Richie Benaud. The man who not so many years earlier had led a renaissance of Australian cricket and who had done so much to lift its image and standard, was now cast as an arch-enemy of the established game.

Now, also, one point was not in dispute: the sparring was over, the in-fighting had begun in earnest.

TEN

The Australians arrived in Nottingham for the Third Test late on Monday, 25 July. Within hours, the bar of their hotel, the Albany, seemed to be flooded with lawyers, both Australian and English, speaking earnestly to some of the tourists.

The word soon got around that Brisbane radio station 4IP was making a determined effort to keep hold of its prize employee, fast bowler Jeff Thomson. Thomson had made world-wide sporting headlines 18 months earlier when he signed a $633,000, 10-year contract with the station, which was working closely with the Queensland Cricket Association to improve the performances of that State's Sheffield Shield team. News of Thomson's signing with the Packer troupe had come as a big shock to station executives, as well as to Thomson's business manager, former Sydney grade cricketer David Lord. Lord was in England, covering the Test series for Sydney television and radio, and had been outspoken in his criticism of the Packer troupe and its likely effect on the game. 4IP had sent its corporate affairs adviser, Mr Frank Gardiner, to England to see if he could persuade Thomson to change his mind about the rebel troupe. Gardiner, a former Queensland University Students' Union president, was now a member of the University Senate, and regarded as a most persuasive man. He had spoken to Thomson in Leicester during the county game a couple of days earlier and was now poised to prise the first chink out of the Packer troupe armour.

But before that there was a Test match to be considered, although anyone wandering into the Albany Hotel in those late July days could be excused for thinking a legal convention was going on, not preparations for an Australia-England cricket

97

Test. The day before, the England selectors had made four changes in the line-up for the Third Test, a surprising number in view of England's 1–0 lead in the series. Out of the 12 were fast bowler Chris Old, unavailable because of a recurrence of an old shoulder injury, opening batsman Dennis Amiss, left-hand batsman Graham Barlow, who had been 12th man at Old Trafford and left-arm opening bowler John Lever, whose form in the first two Tests had been disappointing in view of his good tour to India and Australia.

In, of course, was the controversial Boycott, Derbyshire opening bowler Mike Hendrick, Surrey batsman Graham Roope and Somerset all-rounder Ian Botham. All four had been enjoying excellent seasons and were thoroughly entitled to their places. The surprise was that the usually conservative selectors—Alec Bedser, Ken Barrington, Charlie Elliott and John Murray—had seen fit to include all together.

Boycott's recall had been widely predicted but was still the cause of much discussion in cricket circles. Whatever the personal feelings about him, the dour Yorkshireman was second in the national averages with 977 runs at 61 and in his own opinion, batting as well as ever. This would be his 64th Test, despite the self-imposed exile which had kept him out of Test cricket for three years. The decision to recall him was made easier when Amiss failed with scores of 14 and 11 when he led Warwickshire against the tourists at Edgbaston the previous week.

Hendrick was the logical replacement for Old. The Derbyshire player was fit after several years of injury problems and had taken 8 wickets against the tourists playing for MCC. As well, he led the county averages with 40 wickets at 15.37. Roope was recalled for his first International since the Fourth Test against Australia at The Oval in 1975. He had scored the first century against the Australians on this tour and was the only Englishman, among four county players, to have notched 1000 runs for the season. The talented Botham also deserved his place. With 71 wickets and 670 runs already in the season, he was being widely tipped as the first man to record the elusive double, since Fred Titmus 10 years before. Sometimes referred to as the wild young man of English cricket, Botham was at last responding to discipline. He had spent the winter playing cricket in Melbourne as part of the Whitbread Brewery sponsored plan to give young cricketers more experience and his form had benefited.

In fact, the England team looked far better balanced than it had in the first two games of the series and already it could be seen that the Australians were facing a monumental task to make up lost ground. Chappell, Marsh and Walters faced a formidable task, too, coming up with the right names for the job. There wasn't much they could do—Pascoe was a certainty to play instead of one of the spinners. Robinson had made a determined bid for recall with innings of 70 not out and 137 not out against Warwickshire but the memory of his performances in the First Test was hardly comforting. Serjeant, whose start to the tour had been so promising, had slipped back, failing in three innings since the second Test, although I felt he warranted another chance on the strength of his fighting 81 at Lord's. Of the others, Hughes had four recent failures in county games and Cosier, although starting to find some form, had not improved enough to put pressure on the established batsmen.

The selectors got one shock before they announced their team, after practice on the day before the Test. Ian Davis was hit above the eye by a ball from Mick Malone and had to be taken to hospital for stitching and observation. Later that afternoon, he was passed fit, a relief to the Australians because the right-hand opening bat was just starting to display his best form of the tour. When the team was announced, there was only one change; Serjeant was out and Robinson in. Serjeant could count himself unlucky, but Robinson this time would bat at six, not be sacrificed as an opener as he had been at Lord's. It looked certain that Bright, a disappointment in the Second Test, would be relegated to 12th man for this game, with the tourists taking three fast bowlers onto what looked like a perfect batting wicket at Trent Bridge.

There was much more happening on the Packer front, however, than just the fact that the last of the non-rebels— Serjeant—had disappeared from the Australian team. First, Mr Packer had issued a statement in Sydney, commenting on the ICC meeting. He said: 'It is regrettable, though predictable, that the ICC has taken this stand. All of the players signed for the Supertests were aware of the possibility of such an eventuality, but were prepared to sign on for the series. We have been in contact with all signed players while the threat of banning has been widely canvassed in the press and not one of our players has shown the slightest desire to request a release from his contractual obligations. On the contrary, they have shown greater resolve than ever to make the Supertest series the best cricket in the world. In cutting themselves off from the best players in the world, the ICC and the national cricketing bodies they represent will no longer be in a position to present the finest cricket available. That will now be provided by World Series Cricket through the Supertests.'

Had Mr Packer been in Nottingham the night before the Third Test, he may have wished to alter that statement a little. Frank Gardiner, the Brisbane lawyer, had made no secret of his confidence that he was close to clinching a deal with Thomson that would see him back with Queensland and Australian cricket, and out of the Packer troupe. Mr Gardiner said he had also spoken to West Indian super-batsman Vivian Richards. According to Gardiner, Richards had said he would pull out of the troupe if he was banned from playing county cricket with Somerset. Richards was also reported to have told Mr Gardiner he would be happy to return to Queensland in the next Australian season, under contract to 4IP. Richards was reported to have told the lawyer that he and some others were not prepared to risk their livelihood in cricket if their association with Mr Packer meant they would be banned from playing in England.

At the same time, Mr Lord was talking to another West Indian, Alvin Kallicharran, for whom he had acted as agent in Australia the previous season. The diminutive Kallicharran, reported Lord, was also keen to repudiate his agreement with Mr Packer.

On a night of drama, which had a bar full of journalists hopping from one foot to the other and biting anxiously on their biros, there was one light moment. From Melbourne came the report that the Packer organization was planning to play one or more of its Melbourne games under lights, taking advantage of the new $1 million lighting system recently installed at VFL Park. The twilight games, it was hoped, would start at 3 p.m. and finish at 10 p.m. The formation of the professional troupe games was taking shape rapidly, with several radical changes from normal cricket: the five-day games would be played without a rest day, bouncers would be allowed to tail-end batsmen, and now cricket under lights with yellow balls, instead of the traditional red leather variety.

About midnight, Mr Gardiner emerged from a long discussion with Thomson to announce the news that the explosive fast bowler would not be a part of the Packer package. Mr Gardiner said Thomson had agreed that he had broken his original 4IP contract by signing with Packer. Now Thomson had signed a revised contract with the radio station —which would not be nearly as lucrative as the original—and would be available to play for Queensland and Australia. He would be writing to Mr Packer the next day to explain his withdrawal.

Thomson told reporters that he should never have signed the Packer contract in the first place. Obviously he figured Australian Cricket Board officials would be so thrilled with his defection, they would overlook the small matter of a tour player giving statements to the media. 'I was with a bunch of lads at the time and it seemed OK', the laconic Thomson said, by way of explanation. 'Then, I did not think it would interfere in any way with my cricket career but it has, so I have withdrawn.'

The wall of solidity claimed by the rebels had been breached. There were several Australian cricketers in the room when the Thomson decision was announced, and the general feeling of relief among them was hard to ignore. That feeling was engendered less by personal motives than by the fact that at last someone had made a positive move after weeks of rumour and counter-rumour.

Now, the big question was would Thomson's move open the floodgates? Would there now be a mass exodus of Packer players, who were faced with the prospect of never playing Test or first-class cricket again. Thomson's manager, David Lord, welcomed his client's announcement as a 'major break-through that took a lot of guts'. There was increasing speculation that the next player to make a move toward the exits would be Thomson's longtime friend Len Pascoe. Pascoe had spent several hours talking with his fellow fast bowler before he reached his decision, and had already spoken to Frank Gardiner about the possibility of a move to Queensland.

The ubiquitous Mr Gardiner had not wasted his time in Nottingham. He had arranged a one-year agreement between his radio station and Queensland left-arm fast bowler Geoff Dymock, which ensured that Dymock would remain in the State. Dymock previously had been considering a good offer to move to Tasmania, and play in that State's initial years in the Sheffield Shield competition. Mr Gardiner had also made a lucrative offer for the Western Australian batsman Craig Serjeant to move to Queensland. Serjeant, showing sound judgment for a man who had not yet completed a year in first-class cricket, asked for the offer to be held over until the end of the 1978–79 Australian season, a request that was granted readily. Earlier in the tour, Serjeant had been approached by John Cornell, a principal of J. P. Sport Pty Ltd, to join the Packer troupe, but had given the same answer: if the offer was still open, he would consider it again at the end of the 1978–79 season.

Several other Australian players, and officials, had spoken to Mr Gardiner who made himself available to give advice if required. Another Australian lawyer, former New South Wales spinner Mick Hill, was also prominent in discussions with players.

As news of the Thomson defection spread, the Albany bar filled with Fleet Street journalists and a constantly-ringing bank of telephones. It was hard to believe a Test match was about to start in a few hours. Even before it did, two of the Packer players had affirmed their allegiance to their new master. Dennis Lillee said from Perth: 'There's no way I'll be trying to wriggle out of my contract. We all knew what the consequences might be, and nobody signed without giving it a lot of thought'. His former Western Australian team-mate Ross Edwards was just as strong: 'I've signed with Packer and

I'm right in there behind the series . . . there is no chance I won't be honouring my contract'.

One of the major arguments being raised against the Packer exercise at this time concerned the validity of the contracts signed. Many of the players involved did not have copies of their agreements and their legal advisers were trying desperately to get a glimpse of them. Within a few days of Thomson's decision, copies of the contracts concerning two players were coming under the scrutiny of lawyers representing a variety of interested parties. Several legal men were also stressing the point that under Australian law, the promoting company, J. P. Sport Pty Ltd, was only liable for its paid up capital—at that stage $98—in the case of a breakdown of the troupe or legal action by one or more of the signatories against their employer. No personal guarantees had been issued by the directors of the company, although Mr Packer was to do that soon after, following a request from Ross Edwards.

In Sydney, on 28 July, lawyers representing Mr Packer issued a writ claiming libel against Australian Test selector, Neil Harvey. In June, a similar writ had been issued against me, and my employer, the *Age*, Melbourne.

Against a backdrop of legal activity and undisguised hostility between the warring parties, Greg Chappell won his second successive toss against Mike Brearley on a fine sunny Nottingham day, before a packed Trent Bridge crowd. There was much excitement in the city on this day for apart from the start of a Test match, the Queen was visiting Nottingham as part of her Jubilee Year tour, and it took a long time to travel the two miles from the hotel to the ground near the River Trent. Both teams were to be introduced to the Queen and the Duke Edinburgh after the tea break.

Chappell needed only one glance at the Trent Bridge pitch to know his decision was to bat. Australia left Bright out of its eleven, and England omitted its batsman Graham Roope. For 100 minutes, Chappell had no cause to regret his move. Davis and McCosker gave the side its best start in the series, adding 79 in a confident manner that made their uncertain batting of other games a puzzle all the harder to comprehend.

Willis began in his now accustomed fashion to McCosker,

testing him with two bouncers in his first over. This time, however, McCosker was quickly on the attack, hooking the second safely for four. Mike Hendrick was the more impressive of the England opening bowlers, testing both batsmen with a consistent line and length. Brearley introduced Ian Botham to the Test match bowling crease after only 10 overs, and the 21-year-old Somerset all-rounder induced the first false stroke of the innings when Davis edged his second delivery just wide of the diving Greig at second slip.

The change in attitude of the Australian pair was little short of amazing. In Hendrick's seventh over, Davis went onto the back foot and pulled a short delivery into the temporary scaffold grandstand with ridiculous ease. He was stroking the ball better than he had since arriving in England, and a day after he had received a painful blow over the right eye. The opening 50 came in exactly an hour, off 15.1 overs, with McCosker scoring heavily on the leg-side, his favourite area. For months, English bowlers had restricted him by pitching consistently on or just outside his off-stump, not giving the right-hander the opportunity to work the ball away off his legs. For the first two hours of this Test, Willis, Hendrick, Botham and Greig forgot that theory and McCosker took full advantage.

Davis was the first to depart, however, just when he seemed set for a big score. After he had made 33, he tried to loft Underwood on the on-side, without quite getting to the pitch and gave Botham an easy catch at mid-on. Chappell joined McCosker and the pair carried on merrily enough until lunch when the score was 1/94. McCosker had reached his half-century in Hendrick's last over before lunch when a cover-drive yielded him three runs. It should have been his ninth boundary but Randall made a spectacular sliding save inches from the fence.

If Chappell felt well content with his team's fortunes at lunch, he was hiccoughing by tea. In the two-hour afternoon session, Australia lost 7/72, sliding from a good start into potential disaster with a series of suicidal shots which the Englishmen caught with an alacrity that for years has been missing from their cricket. The debacle began 23 minutes after lunch, just after Chappell had posted the 100. McCosker, who had faced 19 deliveries since the break and not added to his lunchtime score of 51, suddenly flashed at a Hendrick delivery which moved away fractionally and Brearley held the resultant edge confidently at first slip. For the next half hour, Chappell and his new partner, Hookes, proceeded comfortably enough, guiding the total to 131. Then Botham, bowling from the Radcliffe Road end, struck the blow that would have justified his inclusion if he did nothing else. Chappell, on 19, went onto the back foot to try to force a shortish delivery. Instead, it cut back a little, clipped the inside edge of the bat and cannoned into the stumps. The bowler, for whom the Australians had little respect, had suddenly disposed of the one man who could conceivably have torn this attack apart.

Their captain's demise seemed to still the Australians into impotency. Only two runs were added before Hookes sliced at Botham without moving his feet. The ball flew fast, low and wide to the right of Hendrick at third slip. Somehow, the fieldsman managed to throw himself several feet and drag in the catch, two-handed like a soccer goalkeeper—as fine a dismissal as a spectator is likely to see in a lifetime of cricket watching. Australia, 4/133, last man 17, had squandered a good start. Worse was to follow. Walters and Robinson took the score to 153 at which point the innings all but disintegrated. Walters, having reached 11, faced Botham for the first time. Brearley, as if by rote, moved in the two gullies. The batsman, with a great effort of will, allowed the first delivery to pass unhindered. The second left him a little, and that ineffectual jab of the Walters' wrists was again employed, edging the ball low to the left of Hendrick, who held it in both hands. As if to show that Walters wasn't the only man who could surrender so easily, Robinson aimed an horrific swipe at a ball in Greig's next over. It was at least two feet wide of him, and if Robinson, also on 11, was surprised that it travelled into Brearley's outstretched hands, between first and second slip, he had no right to be.

Such situations, 6/153, used to bring out the fighter in Rod Marsh. Not any more; in Botham's next over, he missed one that came back slightly and the only thing that stopped the ball hitting the stumps was his pads. 7/153 and the Australian wicketkeeper was on the way to a pair in his 50th Test match. Botham, on the other hand, was using his medium-paced swerve and cut to enjoy immensely his Test debut. He struck once more before tea, inducing Walker to poke at a ball which bounced, giving slipsfielder Hendrick his third catch of the innings.

Enter Jeff Thomson, once the scourge of England cricket, now accorded a standing ovation, not usually given to a number 10 batsman. I wondered then if those involved in the Packer scheme could understand the sentiments of the paying public, showing their feelings to the man whose decision to quit had been front-page news on most of Fleet Street that morning. Thomson and Kerry O'Keefe held on until tea, when the score was 8/166.

Australia had been wrecked, not only by their own stupidity but by Botham, who had captured in one burst of 34 balls, the wickets of Chappell, Walters, Marsh and Walker, at a cost of only 13 runs. Brilliant catching, by Hendrick and Brearley in particular, had had a large effect on the Australian crash. If ever cricket coaches wanted an example of the importance of fielding, this match was to provide it.

That Australia was able to lift itself from the depths of degradation to a hint of respectability after tea was due to the resolution of O'Keeffe and the brave defiance of Thomson and Pascoe. The trio was responsible for 88 runs being added for the last two wickets, bringing the total to 243 before the innings closed. O'Keeffe finished with 48 not out in 110 minutes and would have been better rewarded with a half century. As at Manchester when he partnered Chappell, he succeeded where his better credentialled team-mates had failed, combining concentration with a realistic appraisal of the position. Both Thomson and Pascoe aimed some heavy and effective blows before departing. Thomson, 21 in a partnership of 41, became Botham's fifth victim of the innings when a big hit ended in Knott's gloves. Just as we were preparing to applaud O'Keeffe's 50, Pascoe, on 20, edged Hendrick to Greig at second slip and the innings was over at four minutes past six. Each of the five bowlers used had been successful, but the energetic and enthusiastic Botham, 5/74 off 20 overs, was by far the most impressive.

Boycott made his return to the Test batting crease to a great roar from the Trent Bridge crowd. He and Brearley had 15 minutes to survive against Thomson and Pascoe, a task achieved with the bonus of eight runs, although Boycott somehow contrived not to face Thomson, who worked up an awesome pace against the helmeted England captain.

It had been England's day with a vengeance—the only highlight for most of the Australians came late in the day when the teams, and officials, were introduced to the Royal couple in front of the Members' Pavilion.

Survival was the name of the game for Boycott and Brearley when play resumed under overcast skies on the second day. Thomson and Pascoe, mindful of their huge task to make up for their batsmen's indiscretions, launched a fearful barrage of pace against the pair for the first hour. And when Walker was introduced into the attack, his intelligent use of the conditions gave both batsmen anxious moments. Only 23 runs came in the hour, Boycott being painfully slow. But his determination was such that it was going to take some extraordinary bowling to prise him from the crease. The constant pressure of the Australian pace trio finally found some success, at the other end. With the opening stand reaching 34 in 86 minutes, Pascoe produced a lifting delivery which Brearley involuntarily jabbed towards gully, where Hookes dived full-length to his left and held a good catch. Three balls later, Woolmer was beaten and lbw to Pascoe for nought, victim of a delivery which seamed back sharply. Now it was Australia's turn to have England on the run at 2/34, including the invaluable scalp of the man who had scored centuries in each of the first two Tests.

The arrival of the local hero, Randall, brought another packed Trent Bridge house to full voice. He was quickly on the attack, pulling a short ball from Chappell viciously to the boundary, bringing up the 50 in the slow time of 105 minutes off 24 overs. Boycott was having his troubles at the other end. When 7, he had snicked Walker just wide off O'Keeffe in the gully. On 11, a forced error from a good Pascoe delivery landed inches in front of the desperately diving Hookes, also in the

107

gully. But these mis-strokes were nothing to the tragedy he was to perpetrate when the score was 52. Boycott pushed a delivery from Thomson firmly down the on-side of the wicket. For reasons unknown, he immediately called for a run and set off. Randall instinctively responded then hesitated as he sensed danger. Thomson, agile in his follow through, moved across quickly, dropped his right hand on the ball, then casually back-handed it to Marsh who smashed the stumps out of the ground with obvious relish, with Randall metres short of safety. It was a selfish and suicidal act by Boycott, and Randall would have been well within his rights to have turned his back on his partner. As it was, he was sacrificed for 13 and the Notts crowd instantly produced a roar of disapproval. Boycott didn't need to be reminded of the error; he stood appalled, his hand covering his face as a forlorn Randall returned to the pavilion.

By lunch, England had struggled to 3/61, Boycott, now 14, had advanced by only 13 runs in the two-hour morning session. Three runs after the break, England lost its fourth wicket when Thomson produced a scorching ball which cut back sharply and removed Greig's middle stump before his bat was halfway through its downswing. The inexperienced Miller arrived in a moment of danger for his side. Fleetingly, he looked like the heaven-sent rescuer as he clipped both Thomson and Walker off his legs to the boundary. But big, burly Len Pascoe wasn't quite finished yet. With the score 82, and Miller's contribution 13, he got a delivery to kick fiercely. Miller, fending for his life, popped the ball in the air for Robinson to dive forward from short leg and hold it jubilantly in both hands. Pascoe now had 3/19 from 9.2 fiery overs and Australia was in the ascendancy.

Five runs later came the incident that many observers, and players, believe cost Australia the series. Boycott, 20 in five minutes short of three hours, was forced to jab hastily at Pascoe. The outside edge travelled thigh high and smoothly, just to McCosker's right at second slip. And that fieldsman, unbelievably, got both hands to it and dropped it. The hands covering the dismayed faces of Chappell and Marsh told the story well enough. It is as axiomatic in cricket as batting or bowling that Geoff Boycott cannot be given a second chance. Had that chance been accepted, England would have been

6/87, chasing 243. But cricket is not a game of 'ifs' and 'buts' as Boycott and his new partner, Alan Knott, were to prove in magnificent splendour over the next four hours.

The situation did not daunt the jaunty Knott. From the moment he arrived at the crease he decided to attack the pace men who had caused his predecessors so much embarrassment. Immediately, he was employing his educated slash high over the heads of the slips cordon to good effect. No matter how much Chappell chased him with a fly-slip or a deep third man, Knott found the gap. Sensing it was his day, he quickly found the confidence to drive, putting the field on the defensive for the first time and forcing the entry of O'Keeffe's ineffectual leg-spin into the attack. The first 50 of the partnership came in only 47 minutes.

Boycott, too, was infected by the insolent aggression of his partner, so much so that he was moved to square drive his first boundary, off Walker, after three and a half hours at the crease. After 234 minutes, he square cut O'Keeffe to bring up his half-century, but received only a muted cheer. He had to do more than that to erase the memory of Randall's sacrifice with this crowd.

Try as he might, Chappell could not wrest the initiative back. Knott brought up his own 50, and the 100 partnership in 112 minutes, caught Boycott in the sixties, then proceeded to match him run for run. This was no innings of luck and chance. It was sensibly applied aggression, born of long experience and determination. Boycott had also thrown mistakes out of his repertoire and was overcoming his own lack of confidence. By stumps, England was 5/242, only one run short of Australia. Boycott was 88 and the day's real hero, Knott, was 87. The stand had so far yielded 160, the bowlers' hearts were broken and the Australian fielding, towards the end, was bordering on the disgraceful—the type that would have had the school third XI kept back an hour until it improved. The thoughts of McCosker did not bear imagining.

The combination of the confident Knott and the dedicated Boycott continued when play resumed on the third day, with some more help from the Australian fieldsmen. Pascoe and Thomson took the new ball immediately, and Robinson at third slip promptly dropped Boycott, 92, off Thomson.

To the great excitement of the crowd, Knott was first to the hundred, cutting Walker for a single, to become the first Englishman to reach three figures against Australia here, since Denis Compton in 1948. Knott had been in command for 203 minutes, hitting 12 fours and a five in a chanceless display as the flamboyant rescuer of his side. Boycott reached his milestone five minutes later when he cut Thomson for two and just made his ground against Walters' return. It was an emotional moment and no one knew it more than the Yorkshire captain who raised his bat high in the air to acknowledge the plaudits of spectators, team-mates and opponents. Despite his lives—at 20 and 92—and the trauma of Randall's run out, he had applied himself to prove to the world what he believed so implicitly himself: that he was the best opening bat in the country. Boycott's century was his fourth against Australia and his 13th in all Tests.

When the tumult had died down, the pair rolled on, increasing the lead over the dispirited Australians. Knott brought up the 200 partnership with that inelegant but effective slice against Pascoe and when the stand had reached 215, it equalled the best for the sixth wicket in England-Australia Tests, set in 1938 by Sir Leonard Hutton and Joe Hardstaff, junior.

The score was 297 when the break finally came. Boycott edged Thomson and McCosker this time held the chance low down, a much more difficult offering than the one he had missed a day earlier. Boycott's 107 had taken him exactly seven hours and included 11 fours. The stand of 215 in 247 minutes had changed the course of the Third Test and, as it turned out, the series.

Knott, small, dark and boundless in energy, carried on unperturbed while his new partner, Botham, frustrated the tourists with a series of wild slashes which rarely connected. All the same, Botham was given every chance to succeed. Chappell, of all people, put down a straightforward slips chance from the third delivery the newcomer faced and when Botham was three, O'Keeffe dropped him in the gully. Thomson was the luckless bowler on both occasions. By lunch, the score was 6/326 with Knott 135, Botham 3 and the lead now 83. Knott's domination ended with the first ball after the break when he slashed at Thomson and Davis, at fly slip, took a good running catch. The innings of 135 had taken only 295 minutes, and included 18 fours and a five. It was Knott's fifth Test hundred, the highest by an England wicketkeeper against Australia—eclipsing Les Ames' 120 in 1934—and during it, he became the first 'keeper to pass 4000 runs in Test matches.

Just to underline his fallibility, Chappell again put down a slips catch, this time shoulder-high to his left from Underwood who had scored 5. Thomson, again the bowler, had formed an unprintable opinion about the standard of his team-mates' catching. Some hard-hitting by Botham took the total to 357 before Pascoe yorked Underwood and Walker did the same to Botham and Hendrick, seven runs later.

England's 364 meant it had a lead of 121, providing Australia with a severe task even to save the Test. Knott and Boycott had performed a miraculous rescue act from the time they had come together at a precarious 5/82 but the Australians, it must be remembered, had put down six chances in the innings, an incredible reversal from the days not so long ago when it seemed anything that flew from the edge was swallowed by the talented slips cordon. Thomson, 3/103 off 31 overs, Pascoe, 4/80 off 32, and Walker, 2/79 off a marathon 39.2 overs, had all strained their hearts and backs, Pascoe even getting a warning the previous evening from Umpire Dicky Bird for persistent short-pitched bowling.

Australia's hopes quickly nose-dived when its second innings began. After 27 minutes and 9 runs, Davis failed to cover a lifting delivery from the vastly-improved Willis, and Greig at second slip swallowed the catch. Chappell opened his account with a fierce drive off Willis, which the acrobatic Randall very nearly turned into the catch of the century. The captain, though, was in no mood for resolute defence. In 37 minutes, he struck 5 fours and 27 runs, sending Australia up to 1/60. But straight after tea Hendrick produced a superb off-cutter which forced Chappell to play across the line, losing his leg-stump in the process. The jubilation of the England team was not hard to understand. Australia was still 61 runs behind with eight wickets standing and its best batsman back in the pavilion.

Now the youthful Hookes joined McCosker for two hours of stern defence before stumps. Neither took risks and by nightfall the score had gone up to 2/112, with McCosker 40 and headed for his second half-century of the match and Hookes 31. Brearley had used five bowlers, Willis, Hendrick, Botham, Underwood and Greig, but they could make no impression on a pitch still full of runs, against a pair who gave an indication that the game could be saved, after all.

When the rest day came, Australia was still 9 runs short of forcing England to bat again and we could sit back to review the events of the last few days. If there had been drama on the field, it wasn't comparable to the intrigue off it.

The Test match was only a few hours old when the telephone rang in the office of Nottinghamshire secretary Group Captain R. G. Wilson. It was an executive of TCN 9 in Sydney, complaining about the presence of an 0-10 network advertisement on the Trent Bridge ground. Channel 9 had paid £150,000 ($240,000) for the right to televize this series live in Australia and didn't feel an opposition advertisement on the ground was playing the game. The Test and County Cricket Board, however, replied that ground advertising was the province of each ground and was not covered in its contract with the Packer television network.

On Friday 29 July, Jamaica's *Daily News* had quoted West Indian captain Clive Lloyd as saying he would 'wait and see' before deciding if he would stay on Packer's books.

During the lunch-break on Saturday, David Lord called a press conference at which he announced the withdrawal of West Indian Alvin Kallicharran from the Packer troupe. Kallicharran, he said, had an option to continue a contract with the petrol company Amoco in Sydney during the next Australian season and he was also looking at the possibility of playing in Queensland. Kallicharran, who had received a $650 signing-on fee when he signed his Packer contract on 2 June, was returning the money as was Thomson, who had received a fee of $11,500 when he signed on in Sydney on 20 April. Lord said Kallicharran had explained that he had been under severe

112

strain in the past few weeks and that he wanted to keep playing for the West Indies, Guyana and Warwickshire. Lord added that he hoped soon to be able to announce the withdrawal of Viv. Richards, another West Indian whose business affairs Lord handled when he played for Queensland in the 1976–77 season.

Also released was the text of a letter from Thomson to J. P. Sport Pty Ltd, telling of his decision to withdraw from the troupe. The letter said, in part: '. . . At the time of my signing, I was not aware of my contractual obligations with my employer, Radio 4 IP of Brisbane. I was told by your representatives that the two would not be in conflict. I was also told, and it was stressed, that your agreement would continue to allow me to play first-grade cricket for Queensland and Australia. Your agreement was to be "additional to" and not "instead of". I have worked far too hard to reach the top of my sport and I did not agree to be banned from representative play.'

Mr Lord also issued a challenge to Mr Packer. 'If Mr Packer is so sure he is right, let him give the players until 31 August to decide their true feelings in the light of what has happened in recent weeks', Lord said.

The news of Kallicharran's defection certainly brought a reaction from Australia. On 31 July, the rest day of the Test, Mr Packer telephoned the West Indian and told him, according to Kallicharran, that there was no possibility of him getting out of his contract. He would be the subject of legal action if he tried. And, added Mr Packer, he was flying to London immediately in a bid to stop players leaving the troupe.

In the meantime, a lawyer drove to Birmingham in an attempt to see the diminutive batsman but was forestalled by Warwickshire captain David Brown, who would not allow the man into the dressing room. Brown was also chairman of the Players' Association, which represented all but one of the county cricketers in England and whose senior officials were opposed to the idea of the Packer troupe. Brown, a former Test fast bowler, said he would not allow Mr Packer, or his representatives, to approach Kallicharran during the county's game against Derbyshire at Chesterfield. The Association would ensure that no additional pressure was placed on the player, Brown promised.

There occurred at that time an incident in the Warwickshire dressing room that reflected the tensions and taut emotions caused by the whole Packer saga. The details must remain confidential but they allowed no credit to any of the participants.

There was another development in the off-field battle, even before the players took the field on the fourth day of the Third Test. Mike Brearley revealed that a wealthy London business-man had come up with a suggestion that could save the five England rebels from being lost to established cricket and could raise substantially the pay structure of England's Test cricketers. The man, former minor county and London club cricketer, Mr David Evans, had already held preliminary talks with TCCB chairman Doug Insole. Under his scheme, he wanted the five rebels, Greig, Underwood, Knott, Snow and Amiss, to be offered the money to buy them out of their Packer contracts. Further, each England player would be sponsored to the tune of $1600 a Test for each Test they played during the next three years. Thirdly, he wanted a pool of some 50 county players picked by the TCCB. Each of the 50 was to be paid a seasonal retainer of $1600 and each player was to be available for selection in Test teams. Mr Evans said the scheme would cost about $775,000, but it would enable regular Test players to earn about $24,800 from the game each season.

There was some confusion as to where the money was coming from. Hurried talks between the TCCB and Mr Evans showed that the sponsorship was dependent upon Mr Evans' office cleaning business winning a substantial contract, the profits from which would be donated to the plan. For a couple of days, Mr Evans was the butt of many derisive comments, but within a fortnight he had arranged substantial and re-volutionary sponsorship for English cricket.

As Hookes and McCosker marched out to resume Australia's second innings, the news reached Trent Bridge that Kerry Packer, accompanied by lawyer Mr Ian Harper, had arrived at Heathrow airport and told reporters: 'I said at the beginning that I would stick with my players when the going

114

got tough. That's why I'm here.' He immediately closeted himself in a luxurious suite in London's Dorchester Hotel with a battery of lawyers. It wasn't long before Mr Packer announced that the next battle would be in the courts.

A huge responsibility rested with Hookes and McCosker as Willis began proceedings to McCosker, who immediately snicked him dangerously close to Greig at second slip. But McCosker quickly wiped off Australia's deficit as he hooked Willis for four, bringing up his own half-century in 184 minutes with 6 fours. The partnership lasted for 79 minutes of the first session as Hookes concentrated on defence. But it ended after 94 runs and 185 minutes when Hendrick's offcutter beat the blond-headed left-hander and umpire Bird gave the bowler the benefit of a dubious lbw decision—dubious, that is, to those of us in the press box with the benefit of the instant replay.

Australia, 3/154, was only 33 runs on and much depended on McCosker's new partner, Walters. Hookes had applied himself well for his 42 runs and his confidence seemed implanted in Walters who began much more assuredly than usual. McCosker, back to his best form after nearly being omitted from the team, was progressing steadily towards his century. The situation, indeed, seemed much rosier for Australia as Walters produced a classical cover-drive from Greig to register the 50 partnership in 75 minutes. Two balls later he tried to repeat the shot against a delivery a trifle shorter and hit it low and hard to an exultant Randall at cover. Australia, 4/204, last man 28.

Robinson joined McCosker while the opening bat reached his century with a lofted hook off Willis that sailed over the boundary for six. He had batted 347 minutes, hitting 10 fours and a six in his fourth Test century and second against England. But McCosker lasted only another 19 minutes before he tried to cut Willis and the top-edge ended up in the hands of Brearley at first slip.

Australia, now 5/240, entered into its habitual middle and late order collapse. Marsh came to the wicket with the look of a man who knows he is predestined for disaster, lasted eight minutes, then pushed forward unsurely to Willis. Greig dived away to his right and the ball stuck in his huge grasp, sending

Marsh miserably back with a pair to his name and Australia 6/240. There was brief respite from Robinson, curbing his natural agression, and O'Keeffe until Underwood pushed through a quicker delivery. Robinson, on the back foot, was unlucky enough to have the ball hit pad before bat and the eagle-eyed Umpire David Constant agreed with the bowler's *sotto voce* appeal. The angular reserve wicketkeeper had made 34 but still failed to give the impression that his batting was of the standard required.

After tea, Walker and O'Keeffe held up the bowlers for 53 minutes and 37 runs, taking the total to 307. Then Willis yorked Walker for 17, and Thomson for a duck six balls later to give him 5/88 for the innings from 26 overs. Underwood finished Australia off at 309 when Pascoe snicked to wide slip, leaving O'Keeffe stranded again on 21. Despite Willis' figures, Hendrick had been the most impressive of the bowlers, while first innings wrecker Botham didn't have a success in 25 overs, which yielded 60 runs.

Australia, once 3/204, had lost its last seven wickets for 105, leaving one day and 26 minutes for England to score the 189 runs for victory. By stumps, they had reached 17 without loss, although Boycott, on 12, had to survive a confident lbw appeal from Thomson's last over of the evening.

The tourists awoke on the morning of the fifth and last day of the Test to read a report in the *Guardian* that Mr Packer was going to ask his players to withdraw from the series against England. The suggestion was quickly, and angrily, denied by Greg Chappell and Ian Chappell. Ian commented: 'He wouldn't do that—every Australian, myself included, would pull out of the troupe if that happened'.

Yet another Packer player, Gloucestershire's South African captain and all-rounder Mike Procter, revealed that he was worried about his position in the troupe. Procter admitted that he was seeking legal advice over the validity of his contract and had agreed to a suggestion from county officials that he sign a new three-year contract to continue with Gloucestershire. Procter said he was well aware that he faced suspension from the county game if he did not withdraw from the troupe by 1 October.

Back at Trent Bridge, Australia's thin chance of drawing the Test evaporated when the day dawned bright and sunny and it became apparent that no disaster, natural or unnatural, had befallen the pitch overnight. Resuming on 0/17, Boycott and Brearley ground inexorably towards the target. There was no haste early, as the Australians appeared mentally and physically incapable of raising the effort needed for a quick breakthrough. If the attack of Thomson, Pascoe, Walker and O'Keeffe was lacking in spirit, the fielding became downright abysmal. One example came when Boycott pushed Walker firmly towards Davis at cover where the ball went untouched between the fieldsman's legs and the batsmen ran two. After 75 minutes, when drinks were taken, the score had advanced by 30 to 0/47. At lunch, it was 0/92 with both batsmen on 45, although there was a palpable difference in their class. Boycott was in total command, eschewing anything that involved risk, and Brearley, at times, seemed surprised at the length of his own occupation of the crease.

Walker emerged after lunch a new bowler, gaining late swing and good movement off the pitch as the conditions became overcast and humid. But he enjoyed little help from his teammates; O'Keeffe, in particular, had no control of line and length. Ian Chappell, who has played in or seen each of the 24 Tests in which O'Keeffe has participated said he had never seen him bowl worse.

The century opening stand—the first of the series—came in 182 minutes off 47.5 overs. Boycott was first to the half-century, in 185 minutes with 6 fours, a magnificent return to the Test arena. Brearley, who had hit 8 fours, followed him 10 minutes later.

The two B's took England to 154—35 runs short of the target —in 221 minutes before the persevering Walker encouraged Brearley to drag a ball onto his stumps as he went for the cut. Brearley, sensing that rain was in the air, sent in Knott to force the pace, but he made only two before he edged Walker and O'Keeffe, diving to his left, held a great gully catch. Greig also failed, losing his stumps to a good Walker delivery as he tried to drive. Walker had conceded only two runs in snaring three wickets as England stumbled slightly to 3/158. But Randall gave his home supporters a few minutes of delight as he raced to 15 then hit the winning four from a loose O'Keeffe delivery.

England had won by seven wickets, in recording its first victory at Trent Bridge since 1930. It was also the first time since 1956 that England had recorded successive Test victories in a series against Australia. Boycott, at 36, had been the hero with scores of 107 and 80 not out in a triumphant return. The cold, hard, bitter fact was that England had thoroughly outplayed Australia in every department of the game, and there was little on which to base any hope for an Australian renaissance. The tourists were a dispirited lot, their fielding in particular having dropped away to an all-time low. Chappell's lieutenants, Marsh and Walters, appeared incapable, or reluctant, to give the support needed. Even the pace bowlers, so often the escape route for Australian teams in trouble, had failed in this match.

England now appeared to have found a well-balanced side, mature enough to accept the return of Boycott as the reappearance of an old friend, youthful and enthusiastic enough to field as well as any England side in memory. Indeed, apart from Boycott, the highlight of this game had been the exceptional catching of Hendrick, Greig and Brearley.

ELEVEN

The Third Test was not two hours dead, and the champagne in the England dressing room still bubbling, when Mr Packer detonated the latest explosion in the cricket war. At a press conference at the Dorchester Hotel, 130 miles from Nottingham, he announced that he would be applying to London's High Court the next day for an injunction against the ICC and the TCCB to prevent them from excluding breakaway players from Test and county cricket. He also indicated that several of his players, including Tony Greig, would be seeking declarations against the ICC, TCCB and MCC that bans would be an unlawful restraint on their rights to play professional cricket. Damages would also be sought 'in respect of recent actions by those bodies'.

Mr Packer also foreshadowed similar proceedings against David Lord, agent of Jeff Thomson and Alvin Kallicharran, alleging that he had wrongfully induced players to break their contracts. Legal actions, of a similar nature, were to be started in Australia, said Mr Packer. Solicitors for the TCCB said later that night that any action by Mr Packer would be defended.

At the press conference, Mr Packer told reporters: 'This is the first ball of a five-day match. It's just a start. Whatever happens there, we will come to a conclusion at a later date which will show that the ICC has no right to stop players earning a living with anyone else if they choose to. I'm made out as villain because I'm having the effrontery to use the courts to protect myself. I don't follow the logic of it, but I believe I am going to win.'

Court No 9 at the Royal Courts of Justice building in the Strand was crowded when proceedings opened before Chan-

119

cery Division Vacation Judge, Mr Justice Slynn the next morning, 3 August. The historic old building, only yards from the start of Fleet Street, had been the setting for many celebrated cases, but this challenge to the authority of the cricket establishment was unique.

Counsel retained by Mr Packer, Mr Robert Alexander QC and Mr Andrew Morritt QC, sought temporary injunctions in three writs. Two of the writs were brought by Mr Packer's company J. P. Sport Pty Ltd—promoters of the proposed Packer troupe matches—one against the International Cricket Conference and the other against Mr David Lord. The third action was brought by former England captain Tony Greig, and two other county cricketers John Snow and Mike Procter against the ICC and the Test and County Cricket Board.

Mr Patrick Milmo represented the TCCB and Mr Oliver Popplewell QC the MCC. Mr Popplewell at first argued that the MCC was not involved but was over-ruled. Mr Lord was not represented or present and the three cricketers were not in court. But among the cricket authorities who were there was ICC secretary Jack Bailey and TCCB secretary Donald Carr. After a day of hearing arguments by counsel for both sides, Mr Justice Slynn said he would hand down judgement the following afternoon.

Mr Alexander said in his address: 'In the last few days, and particularly since 26 July, the situation has developed with great speed and all the indications which are available to us suggest that there is to be taken on Friday, or at least considered on Friday, a step which will have the gravest repercussions for professional cricketers and their existing contractual relationships.' (He was referring to the TCCB meeting, scheduled for 5 August, in which the Board was to announce its policy on those signed with the Packer troupe.) He explained that J. P. Sport, a company incorporated in Australia, had contracts with about 50 leading cricketers with a view to holding a series of matches over the next few years.

The TCCB was the body responsible for the domestic administration of cricket in Britain while the ICC was responsible for the administration of international cricket.

Mr Alexander said the action was being brought against Mr

120

Lord because of his 'avowed intention' to induce all players to break contracts signed with J. P. Sport.

The issues raised by the actions, said Mr Alexander, were of grave legal importance and involved such questions as whether cricketers should have a measure of freedom to decide for whom and where and upon what terms they would play. It also raised the issue of whether the TCCB and the ICC were entitled to bring every pressure possible to bear upon cricketers to break existing contracts with J. P. Sport.

Later, Mr Alexander said: 'There is no suggestion that the contracts entered into between those players and J. P. Sport were otherwise than perfectly lawful contracts'.

Mr Packer said in a sworn statement read to the judge by Mr Alexander that cricketers had long been grossly underpaid for Test appearances compared with sports like golf, tennis and football. When the cricketers signed for him, it was stressed that they were engaging in a serious business enterprise and the highest standards would be expected of them, on and off the field. It was never intended to interfere with the English domestic season. It was explained that the Packer matches would be scheduled to start after the end of the English season and terminate before the next.

Mr Alexander said that J. P. Sport had so far put about $4 million into launching the project. Any award of damages at the end of the legal dispute would be inadequate to compensate for the loss of profits, goodwill and reputation Mr Packer would suffer if the venture failed, he claimed. It was therefore a matter of extreme urgency that injunctions should be granted.

Mr Popplewell, on behalf of the MCC, argued that cricket authorities would not be acting in restraint of trade, or inducing breach of contract, merely by telling a player that, because he had contracted with Mr Packer, he would not be eligible to play in county cricket. Nor would they be inducing a breach of contract merely by saying to a player that he already had a contract with somebody else and ought to fulfil that obligation first, he said.

'The idea of players being prevented by a board of control from playing is far from the truth. Mr Packer has bound them hand and foot to play for him for the next three years and they cannot play for anybody else unless he consents', Mr Popplewell said. 'What this dispute is about has nothing whatever to do with English cricket. It is about the fact of what Mr Packer wanted.'

Legal argument lasted all day before Mr Justice Slynn adjourned the case until the next afternoon for decision. Court 9 was again packed to over-flowing when the bewigged, red-sashed judge resumed the cases at precisely 2 p.m. on 4 August.

The High Court refused to grant the injunctions against the ICC and TCCB sought by J. P. Sport and players Greig, Snow and Procter. But the injunction sought by J. P. Sport against David Lord was granted to last until the Court sat again in seven days. The injunction restrained Mr Lord from 'wrongfully inducing players to break their contracts with Packer'. Mr Lord was in court to hear the verdict, although he had not been represented at the hearing the day before.

In a 40-minute reading of his decision, Mr Justice Slynn said he was ordering a speedy trial of the matters which he said would probably be held late in September. In his judgement, Mr Justice Slynn said, he had taken into account an assurance by the TCCB counsel that no decision would be made at its meeting the next day that would be implemented before 1 April 1978. Mr Justice Slynn also said he had taken into account an ICC assurance that it would take no further action before a trial of the matter was finalized.

As the plaintiffs and defendants left the courtroom, TCCB secretary Donald Carr said he was satisfied with the outcome. 'It means our meeting tomorrow can go ahead as planned', he said. The general feeling in cricket circles was that, although he had not been granted the injunctions, Mr Packer had at least won the skirmish on points. He now had a stay of execution on the player bans until the case was tried.

In Sydney the day before, J. P. Sport Pty Ltd had issued a writ against three members of the Australian Cricket Board. The writ was taken out through the Federal Court of Australia. It was issued against the secretary of the ACB, Mr Allan Barnes; the chairman, Mr Robert James Parish; and an agent and delegate for the Board at a meeting of the ICC in London on 26 July, Mr Tim Charles John Caldwell.

The plaintiff company's claim was for:

1 The declaration that Mr Caldwell and the members of the ACB had acted in contravention of a section of the Trade Practices Act.
2 An injunction restraining the defendants by themselves, their servants or agents, from engaging in conduct that hinders or prevents the supply of services by third persons to the plaintiff company.
3 An interim injunction restraining the defendants by themselves, their servants or agents from giving effect to or implementing certain resolution.

In a statement of claim, J. P. Sport was described as a trading corporation. The statement said that the company was engaged in the business of promoting, organizing and conducting professional sporting events and plans to promote and organize a number of series of professional cricket matches in Australia and elsewhere commencing 1 September, in 1977, 1978 and 1979. The statement also said: 'In addition to being sued in their personal capacities, the defendants are sued on behalf of all members of the board'. The writ had not been heard by early October, 1977.

Now it was no longer a war of words and threats. The battle between the Packer troupe and the cricket establishment had reached the courts. With each writ issued, and injunction sought, the sounds of compromise grew more distant.

TWELVE

The most elusive single element in the whole Packer saga, since the story broke on 9 May, had been the contracts signed by the players. Very few, if any, of the players had been allowed to keep copies after signing. John Snow, Mushtaq Mohammed, Jeff Thomson, Alvin Kallicharran, Ian Chappell, Ian Davis, David Hookes, Mick Malone and Mike Procter all said their contracts had been held by Packer troupe officials in Sydney after they were signed.

The very scarcity of the agreements made it difficult for lawyers, acting on behalf of some players and officials, to give advice. Eventually, during the Trent Bridge Test, copies of several contracts were produced and lawyers were able to study them. Two legal men described one of the contracts to me as 'unconscionable'. The *Daily Mail* of 2 August printed in full a copy of one player's contract. A legal expert, who examined the contract at the *Daily Mail*'s request, commented: 'It seems harsh and authoritarian. It appears to give the promoter virtually unlimited powers over the players who have signed.'

Even Mr Packer admitted the contracts were tough. In an interview on Yorkshire TV on 4 August he said: 'I make no apologies for the fact that the contract is tough. I told every player "this is a tough contract and you'll do as you're damn well told".'

Because the signing of the contracts was the catalyst for the greatest upheaval in cricket history, the wording of one of the contracts is reproduced here. This is a contract signed by one of the 51 players in the troupe. His name, amounts of money involved, and date of signing, have been omitted at his request.

Agreement made this . . . day of . . . 1977 between J. P. Sport

Pty Limited a company incorporated in the State of New South Wales and having its registered office at 8 Kippax Street near Sydney in the said State (hereinafter referred to as 'the promoter') of the one part and ... (hereinafter referred to as 'the player') of the other part whereas:

A   the promoter is engaged in the business of promoting organising and conducting professional sporting events and plans to promote, organise and conduct a number of series of professional cricket matches in Australia and elsewhere in the seasons as hereinafter defined.

B   each series will comprise up to 65 play days devoted to six matches described as 'Test Matches' (each being of up to five days duration) six limited over matches (each being of two days duration) and as yet an undecided number of other matches, all of which matches in a series shall together constitute a tour.

C   the player has offered to play in matches of the tours hereinafter specified and as the promoter hereafter may from time to time require and generally to participate as a playing member in each of those tours.

Whereby it is agreed and declared that the promoter engages the player to provide his services and the player agrees to provide his services to the promoter for the purposes for the term and on and subject to the terms and conditions herein set forth, that is to say:

1   Where herein appearing the expression: 'season' shall mean the period commencing on 1 September of a year and ending on 30 March in the next calender year and each season shall be identified by the year in which the month of September falls.'tour' shall mean and include the duration of that part or parts of a season as shall be specified by the promoter from time to time and the matches to be played in that period. 'venue' shall mean the cricket ground selected by the promoter for the playing of a match of a tour.

2   The term of this agreement shall be for ... calendar months commencing on the first day of September 1977 (hereinafter referred to as 'the said term').

3   The player undertakes and agrees that during the said term:

(a) he will in each tour of the 1977, 1978 and 1979 seasons:

   (1) on the direction of the promoter unless prevented by illness or accident or for any other reason satisfactory to

125

the promoter play in the matches of a tour for which he is chosen by the promoter and will at all times play to the best of his ability and skill provided however that the player shall not be required to play for more than 65 days in the aggregate in any tour (apart from the two days referred to in clause 4(b) hereof but subject always to the provisions of clause 5 hereof).

(2) punctually attend at such times and places as the promoter may direct for the purpose of playing the aforesaid matches or for practice or otherwise as the promoter may require.

(3) be at the venue at all times dressed in cricket uniform ready to commence play at least 15 minutes before the time for the commencement of play each day and thereafter throughout each such day.

(4) at all times so conduct himself as to enhance the business and reputation of the promoter in promoting professional cricket in Australia and elsewhere and will not do or omit to do anything whereby the good name and reputation of the promoter or of any of its employees or of himself or of any other player taking part in a tour will or may be likely to be brought into disrepute or ridicule.

(5) at all times in a tour obey the directions and conform in all respects to the arrangements for the conduct of a tour made by the promoter.

(6) keep himself physically fit at all times and not commit any act or be guilty of any act or conduct calculated to render him unfit to play in or incapable of playing in any match of a tour.

(7) during the whole of each tour stay and reside at such places as the promoter shall from time to time select and will not without the consent of the promoter stay or reside elsewhere.

(8) at all times comply with and will not breach such regulations as may for the time being be in force at any venue.

(9) travel between venues and otherwise whilst on tour as a member of a team and otherwise as directed by the promoter.

(10) participate by personal appearances in team group photographs and television programmes and/or adver-

126

tisements (live and pre-recorded) for tour news and promotional and publicity purposes.

(11) take part in cricket coaching clinics for five days as the promoter may from time to time direct by giving the benefit of his skill and knowledge as a cricketer to members of the public attending such clinics.

(b) he will not:

(1) play in any cricket match other than a match of a tour without the consent in writing of the promoter first had and obtained.

(2) appear on radio or TV nor grant interviews for nor write or submit articles for publication in any newspaper or magazine or periodical except in each case as first authorised in writing by the promoter.

(3) give endorsements for goods of any nature nor allow his name or photograph to be used for promotional or advertising purposes except as first authorised in writing by the promoter.

4 The promoter undertakes and agrees that during each tour it will:

(a) pay to the player a reasonable allowance per each day of the tour to cover his cost of accommodation and meals and will pay an economy-class air travel between venues and transportation between accommodation and venue but excluding freight or charges on luggage in excess of that determined by the promoter and the player undertakes to pay any such excess.

(b) organise and conduct a two-day limited over match in Australia and pay the whole of the cash receipts from that game (after deduction of all reasonable and actual expenses) to a players provident fund to be established by a committee to be constituted by a nominee of the promoter and two nominees to be appointed by the majority of those players who take part in the 1977 season tour and being generally for the benefit of those players and of players in future tours and being more particularly for the purposes and to the extent and on and subject to such rules as regards membership of the fund entitlements thereunder and the nature of the benefits to be provided by that fund as that committee as then or thereafter constituted shall from time to time decide but so that the moneys paid to that fund shall not be or deemed to be assets of the promoter.

5 The player acknowledges that he is aware that the promoter plans to promote organise and conduct from time to time series of matches outside Australia and he undertakes and agrees at the direction of the promoter to participate as a player in all or any of those series as shall be conducted during the said term subject to the promoter:

(a) providing economy class air travel from and on return to his normal place of residence and

(b) the other provisions of this agreement where applicable being applied to that tour.

6 The promoter will pay to the player as the full and only moneys payable to him under or pursuant to this agreement:

(a) for his participation in each tour in Australia a total fee of . . . being at the day rate of . . . for each of the aforesaid 65 play days. The said fee shall be payable as to . . . on the day of the signing of this agreement, as to a further . . . immediately following the completion of the third Test match or on the . . . day of . . . in that season (whichever shall be the earlier) and as to . . . on completion of the tour.

(b) for each tour outside Australia a total fee in the same amount and payable in the same way as set out in paragraph (a) above provided however that if the number of play days in that tour differs from 65 then the said total fee shall be reduced or increased by deducting therefrom or adding thereto an amount to be calculated at the rate of 2 per cent of the said total fee for each day of difference as the case may be. The player will also receive a 15 per cent share of the gate receipts after deducting all actual costs from matches in which they have appeared to be divided equally between players involved in those matches.

7 The player except with the approval of the promoter shall not in any manner whatsoever give any information concerning matters connected with a tour or his connection with the promoter under this agreement or concerning this agreement to the Press or any member or representative thereof or to any broadcaster or any broadcasting or television station operator or any representative thereof.

8 For each tour:

(a) the promoter shall appoint a tour principal and a tour manager.

(b) the tour manager shall have control of the players on

Tireless Max Walker was the unlucky bowler of the series. Here umpire David Constant turns down a confident lbw appeal against Ian Botham, Third Test.   Patrick Eagar photo.

The end of Rick McCosker's fighting century at Trent Bridge, caught Brearley off Willis for 107. Richie Robinson is the non-striker.   Patrick Eagar photo.

In July the huge concrete tubs in which the controversial Packer cricket pitches were to be prepared, arrived outside VFL Park, Melbourne. *Age* photo.

Sharp close-in catching was a highlight of England's Ashes win. Tony Greig shows his style in dismissing Ray Bright in the second innings of the Fourth Test. Patrick Eagar photo.

Geoff Boycott, padded chest and all, raises his bat high to acknowledge the crowd's salute after he had scored his 100th first-class century in England's first innings of the Fourth Test at Headingley.   Patrick Eagar photo.

Test cricket can be an anguishing experience as Ray Bright discovered in the Fourth Test. His feelings were apparent here as a poker-faced Bill Alley no-balled him, shortly after the pair had clashed.
Patrick Eagar photo.

Thousands of excited Yorkshire fans besieged the English dressing room after the Ashes had been regained in the Fourth Test at Headingly.
Patrick Eagar photo.

England captain Mike Brearley caused much comment with the plastic skull-cap he wore against the fast bowlers. Here he ducks under a Thomson bumper during the Fifth Test at The Oval.   Patrick Eagar photo.

The Fifth Test was Greg Chappell's last. His distinguished Test batting career finished when Derek Underwood caught and bowled him for 39. Patrick Eagar photo.

Doug Walters' last Test innings in England was, like so many before it, disappointing. Bob Willis sent his off-stump sprawling and Walters departed, still without a century in a Test in England. Patrick Eagar photo.

Kerry Packer arrives at
London's High Court
in August for the hearing of
cases in which his company
J. P. Sport Pty Ltd,
and three players, sought
injunctions against the Test
and County Cricket Board and
the International Cricket
Conference.   AP photo.

Former Test umpire
Jack Collins, just signed up
with the Packer organization,
tests the artificial pitches being
grown in a hothouse outside
VFL Park, Melbourne,
in October.   *Age* photo.

tour and all necessary arrangements respecting accommodation travelling and medical attention shall be made by him.

(c) the tour manager shall be empowered to appoint team captains and select players to take part in matches.

(d) the tour manager shall be authorised in the name of the promoter to give or make such directions authorisations decisions and consents and to express such requirements as the promoter by this agreement is empowered to give or make and any direction decision or requirement so made by the tour manager shall for the purposes of this agreement be a direction decision or requirement of the promoter and be binding on the player.

(e) notwithstanding anything herein before contained the tour principal shall be authorised and empowered to give or make any direction authorisation decision or consent and to express such requirements as the promoter by this agreement is empowered to give or make and any direction decision or requirement so made by the tour principal shall for the purposes of this agreement be a direction decision or requirement of the promoter and be binding on the player and to the extent that any direction authorisation decision consent or requirement may be given by the tour principal shall conflict with any direction authorisation decision or consent made or given by the tour manager then the direction authorisation decision consent or requirement as the case may be made or given by the tour principal shall prevail over that made or given by the tour manager.

9   In the event that during a tour the player shall fail for any reason beyond his control to observe or fulfil any of his obligations hereunder including (but without limiting the generality) any failure to obey the directions decisions or requirements of the promoter or any misconduct which in the decision of the promoter is contrary to the well being of the tour then the promoter shall be at liberty forthwith and without notice and in its absolute discretion to terminate this agreement with the player and thereupon the player shall not have any claim to any compensation or other payment or to receive from the promoter any of the moneys referred to in clause 6 of this agreement except to the extent that any moneys paid or payable to him under that clause shall be less than the amount to be calculated by multiplying the day rate

referred to in clause 6 by the number of play days which have expired at the date of such termination or as an alternative to termination the promoter shall be entitled to withhold either permanently and for such time as it may decide so much of any moneys payable or to become payable by the promoter to the player hereunder as the promoter shall from time to time decide as a penalty and any moneys so withheld may be retained by the promoter and be dealt with by it on the completion of that tour in such manner as it may decide and the player agrees that any decision by the promoter to terminate this agreement as aforesaid or to impose a penalty as aforesaid or as to the justification for termination or the nature or amount of the penalty shall be binding on the player and shall be finally subject however to the right of the player within seven days after the date of decision of the promoter to appeal to the tour principal by written notice setting out the grounds of such appeal and the decision of the tour principal on such appeal shall be final and binding in all respects as the player doth hereby agree and the player further agrees that any termination or imposition of penalty aforesaid shall not be in derogation of any other legal rights or remedies available to the promoter.

10 This agreement and the benefit thereof shall be assignable by the promoter.

11 This agreement shall be governed by and shall be construed in accordance with the laws of the State of New South Wales and shall be subject to the jurisdiction of the courts of that State.

In witness whereof the parties hereto have set their hands the day and year first herein before written.

Like most contracts, many of its clauses are difficult to understand. Clause 6 concerned several of the legal experts who studied it in Nottingham. 'The promoter will pay to the player as the full and only moneys payable to him under or pursuant to this agreement.' At that stage, the promoter, J. P. Sport had a paid up capital of $98 and was liable for only that amount. Once he arrived in London on 1 August, however, Mr Packer moved quickly to rectify that position. On 2 August he was able to announce that most players had been given personal guarantees from his television empire for the amounts due over the next three years. And that was estimated to be in excess of $3 million.

THIRTEEN

It was proving well-nigh impossible for cricketers, or cricket observers, to concentrate on the game, even though the vital Fourth Test at Leeds was only a few days away. On 4 August, the British Broadcasting Corporation hinted that it could be screening some of the Packer games in the United Kingdom during the Australian summer. The BBC's head of sport, Cliff Morgan, admitted: 'We are always interested in good sporting productions. We don't know the costs yet or whether our times will coincide with the Packer matches'. To cushion the shock for the Establishment, he added: 'We have a good relationship with the Test and County Cricket Board and certainly don't want to jeopardize that. We wouldn't go behind their backs.'

The TCCB met at Lord's on 5 August to consider, among other things, what policy it would take on county players involved with the troupe. Decisions were made relating to a ban on those players, but no statement was made. Board officials would seek legal advice before making a public statement before the start of the Fourth Test on 11 August. But the TCCB did advise its four-man selection panel that the England Test team must continue to be picked on merit.

Organizers for World Series Cricket—the original promoter J. P. Sport had undergone a name change—announced the names of two umpires for their series, Peter Enright of Queensland and Gary Duperouzel of Western Australia. Enright, a former Test umpire, had retired four years earlier from the first-class game and Duperouzel had been WA's leading man in white for the past three years.

And what of the Australian tourists? After Nottingham, they had travelled 300 kilometres north to Sunderland where they really managed to hit rock bottom—defeat for the first time by the Minor Counties, in a two-day game. The game, a non-first-class fixture really didn't matter, but the team's morale, already dangerously low, was further impaired. To add injury to insult, acting captain Doug Walters was struck unconscious while batting in the second innings and had several stitches inserted in a nasty wound under his chin.

So the party returned to Manchester for the game against Lancashire, having its worst county season for many years. More importantly, it was the last chance for several players to press for Test places. Australia, already down two Tests in the rubber, had to win the remaining two to draw the series and retain the Ashes. To achieve that, was going to require a remarkable reversal of form and spirit. There was a glimmer of hope at Manchester where the Australians won by seven wickets in an exciting finish. There were good batting performances by Cosier, 23 and 66 as an opener, Hughes, 89, Robinson, 52, and Chappell 70 not out in a whirlwind second innings. As well, Thomson, Malone and Dymock all showed good form and Bright took five second innings wickets. The trip to Leeds, then, was a little cheerier than most on this tour.

England's selectors had shown themselves to be well content with the efforts of their warriors; the squad for the Fourth Test was unchanged. Yorkshire fast bowler Chris Old was again unavailable because of his shoulder injury, but had he been fit it would have been hard to squeeze him in following the success of Hendrick and Botham at Trent Bridge. There was more good news for the England players. The much-criticized businessman Mr David Evans had come up with a scheme that would see each of the players taking part in the Fourth and Fifth Tests, getting $1600 a game in sponsorship. Mr Evans had convinced several business houses to join him in the venture, and the money was to be handed over to England captain Mike Brearley at Leeds. Brearley, who was fighting hard to achieve any sort of compromise between the established game and the Packer version, had resisted a suggestion from the group of business men that the Packer players, Greig, Underwood and Knott be left out of the sponsorship.

In the West Indies, the Board of Control there announced on

7 August, that it would abide by the ICC decision to ban players. Chairman Jeff Stollmeyer said: 'The 14 West Indians involved have until 1 October to make up their minds'.

The England Players' Association heard on 9 August that Mr Packer had turned down a request to meet the Association to discuss his plans. Packer said he planned to return to Australia before such a meeting could take place, but yielded under pressure from president, Mr John Arlott, and agreed to meet the Association executive the next week. The movements of Mr Packer were causing excitement in England and when the television chief asked for, and was granted, a place in the Australian Press team to play the English Press on the rest day of the Fourth Test, the game suddenly took on the status of a Supermatch.

The Australians, quartered at a magnificent hotel, the Post House, at Bramhope, overlooking the Yorkshire moors on the outskirts of Leeds, entered into their preparation for the Fourth Test with obvious relish. Poor accommodation had dogged the team for much of the tour; it was probably only a minor factor in their poor performances, but Chappell has seen fit to deliver a blast against many of the team's quarters late in July. 'Most of the hotels are so bad, they are depressing. They have had a bad effect, especially on the younger team members', he said. The captain laid the blame squarely on the Australian Cricket Board. 'Perhaps because the ACB gave the players a pay rise recently, they cut costs in other areas', he said acidly. He singled out hotels in Scarborough, Chesterfield and Northampton as the worst. 'The rooms did not have baths, paint was peeling from walls and ceilings; it was appalling.' In fact, the Scarborough hotel had been fined heavily for inadequate health measures in its kitchen the day the Australians left and two weeks later was forced to close down because of lack of patronage. Chappell pointed out that teams touring Australia had first-class accommodation. 'And, if they don't like it, they can change', he said, referring to a move in hotels made by the Pakistanis in Melbourne last summer. Chappell was quite justified in his criticism. Many of the team's hotels were third rate.

There was a definite uplifting in team spirit before the Leeds

133

Test. Senior players at last became active in their off-field attitude to their team-mates. Now, Walters, Marsh, Chappell and Walker could be seen talking earnestly to younger, less experienced players. And there was a zest at the nets that had been missing since the start of the tour. Unfortunately, the selectors retained their policy of picking their most experienced team for the important games. I felt this was a major flaw in the thinking of Chappell, Marsh and Walters throughout the series. In opting for the more experienced Davis, Robinson, indeed Walters himself, they ignored the claims of batsmen, especially Hughes and Serjeant. Serjeant played in the first two Tests, scored 81 at Lord's and was left out of the Third and Fourth games. Davis, whose form had been consistently poor and Robinson, whose batting never reached Test standard, were given too many opportunities to fail.

There would be no second chances after this Test; Australia had to win to stay in the Ashes fight. A loss, or a draw, would see the trophy back in England's possession. It seemed to this observer that the time had come for Australia to gamble on youth; relying on experience had not proved a particularly successful policy in the previous two Tests. It was not to be. After Len Pascoe had proved his fitness at the tourists' final practice session—he was suffering from a groin strain and soreness in thigh muscles—Greg Chappell announced an unchanged 12 for the Fourth Test. It could well have been one of the last sides Chappell would have a hand in selecting. A day earlier, he had heard that the Queensland Cricket Association had sacked him as a State selector because of his Packer affiliation. The Australian and Queensland captain had reacted unhappily: 'There are a lot of narrow-minded people who take into consideration what has happened in the past three months rather than the past three years. I don't know what went on at the meeting, but some people sure have short memories', commented a bitter Chappell. Perhaps surprisingly, one of the men who wanted Chappell retained was QCA Executive chairman Norm McMahon. But Mr McMahon was in England as assistant manager—treasurer to the touring side.

Despite the unchanged squad, there was certain to be one difference in the side when the Test began. Left-arm spinner

Ray Bright would play, ahead of Kerry O'Keeffe. Bright's form in the Lancashire game had been enough to tip the scales in his favour. O'Keeffe's bowling had been a big disappointment; in three Tests he had taken only three wickets for 305 at the extravagant average of 101.6. But he did lead the batting averages with 125 runs at 62.5 and his doughty batsmanship was commendable enough for him to be tipped as a possible opener before the Third Test.

England had its problems, too. Bob Woolmer reported to Leeds with an infected finger in his right hand, and Somerset opener Brian Rose was despatched northwards to stand by. Rose, a left hander, had hit a century against the tourists and his subsequent county form had made him a Test contender.

On the eve of the Test, the TCCB announced its decision regarding Packer signatories who were also involved in county cricket. Pending the outcome of the High Court case, the Board would impose a two-year ban on any player who took part in the Packer games, the ban to become effective when the player, or players, had finished playing their last game with the rebels. In effect, the TCCB decision meant that most Packer players would be out of county cricket for five years, since the majority had signed three-year contracts. The 17 players affected on 10 August were: Tony Greig, John Snow and Imran Khan (Sussex), Alan Knott, Derek Underwood and Asif Iqbal (Kent), Mike Procter and Zaheer Abbas (Gloucestershire), Barry Richards, Gordon Greenidge and Andy Roberts (Hampshire), Eddie Barlow (Derbyshire), Viv. Richards, Joel Garner (Somerset), Mushtaq Mohammed (Northampton-shire), Clive Lloyd (Lancashire) and Collis King (Glamorgan). The TCCB decision differed from the ICC ban in only one important aspect: it offered the players the chance to return automatically to county cricket after serving the suspension, if the counties were prepared to sign them.

On the same day, the Packer organization in Sydney announced the dates for the proposed troupe games over the summer. The dates were the same as those published in the Melbourne newspaper *Sunday Press* two weeks earlier. There were scheduled as well 15 one-day games, a country competition and three night matches.

135

Despite all this, the biggest talking point in cricket-mad Leeds was whether Geoff Boycott could use the occasion of the Fourth Test match, on his home ground in front of an adoring army of spectators, to complete his century of centuries in first-class cricket. The Yorkshire captain's 107 at Trent Bridge had been his 98th, and earlier in the week he had chalked up his 99th, against Warwickshire at Birmingham. Only 17 men before him had registered the century—John Edrich became number 17 earlier in the season—and none of them had achieved the milestone in a Test match. Such was the volume of money to say he could, that Ladbroke's were forced to offer the ridiculously short quote of 3/1 by the time Brearley won the toss and opted to bat. Boycott might have been unpredictable and moody as far as the south of England and the rest of the world was concerned, but in Yorkshire he could do no wrong . . . as he was to prove.

The Headingley pitch looked an excellent one for batsmen when Boycott and Brearley walked out to open the England innings. There was no sign of the fungus fusarium that had ruined the 1972 Australians and the security here now was such that there was little likelihood of the vandalism that had destroyed the 1975 Test. Australia, predictably, had left O'Keeffe out of its 11 and England had given Roope his chance, in place of Miller whose two innings in the previous Tests had yielded only 19 runs.

The match was only three balls old when the Australians struck first blood. Brearley, without a jot to his name on the scoreboard, played tentatively forward to Thomson and Marsh ecstatically threw the ball heavenwards. Brearley's indignant glare at the Australian wicketkeeper did not fool umpire Lloyd Budd, whose raised finger meant England was 1/0. Woolmer, who had passed a fitness test on his injured finger before the start of play, joined Boycott and the pair proceeded cautiously. Chappell preferred Walker as Thomson's opening partner, but the experiment was a failure as the big Victorian had trouble finding his rhythm. Despite the batsmen's lack of haste, 42 runs came in the first hour off 11 overs. Boycott showed his first real aggression shortly after, despatching a short Walker delivery past point, and then the mishap the tourists dreaded most, happened again. Boycott, probing at a good Walker outswinger, got a thin edge. Marsh dived desperately to his right, got the ball in his glove and could only watch in horror as it bounced out as his body hit the ground. Dropped at 20 in the Third Test, Boycott had gone onto to a century; dropped at 22 here, he was to punish the Australians even more severely.

Four runs later, another incident involving Boycott convinced the tourists that the fates were set against them; Pascoe got a delivery to kick sharply from the Members' end, forcing Boycott to fend hurriedly. The Australians rose as one man as the ball disappeared into Marsh's gloves. They could hardly believe their eyes as Budd remained unmoved by their entreaties. Boycott rubbed his elbow as if trying to give an impression, but anyone who saw the television replay had to believe that the umpire may have been a little astray in his judgement.

That's cricket though, and Boycott and Woolmer carried on until lunch time with the score 1/77. Only five runs were added after the break before Thomson struck again. Woolmer, on 37, sparred at a good length delivery which ended in the hands of Chappell, crouching low at first slip. The new batsman, Randall, was in aggressive mood, in direct comparison to Boycott. Randall cut Thomson viciously for four, brought up the 100 in 161 minutes by on-driving Walker for three, then raced to 20 in 27 minutes as he despatched a Pascoe full toss to the boundary. His avarice for runs was his undoing then, as he played across the line trying to force Pascoe on the on-side and Umpire Alley agreed wholeheartedly with the appeal. England 3/105, could be considered to be in a shaky position as Greig strode out to join Boycott in a decisive rescue mission. Greig had adopted a more defensive outlook on his batting this northern summer, but soon produced the shot of the day, hooking Pascoe with infinite ease over fine leg for six.

Boycott grafted to his half-century in 177 minutes, surprisingly with 8 fours, amid violent cheering from the packed outer terraces, who began to sense that their dearest wish would come true. Greig turned Pascoe for a single to bring up the 150 in 215 minutes, then launched a furious assault on Thomson,

137

repeatedly driving him through the covers. Boycott, too, began to display a wide-ranging repertoire, a back-foot drive to the fence off Walker being the highlight.

There was more drama when the local hero had reached 75. He tried to turn Bright on the leg-side, Marsh took the ball cleanly and the entire Australian team launched a raucous appeal. Bright, mid-way through a celebratory dance, suddenly realized that Umpire Alley had no intention of giving the batsman out. The young Victorian spoke several unkind words, and as Alley proffered his cap, snatched it away, still speaking in a less than friendly manner. It was too much for the former New South Wales State player, Alley. No mean man with an epithet himself, he waved a warning finger at the angry Bright, then motioned for Chappell to intervene. The Australian captain raced from slip and admonished Bright for several minutes. At the end of the dialogue, Alley indicated his satisfaction and no further action was taken.

The Australians, to a man, were adamant later that Boycott was out. But such leg-side catches at the wicket are always difficult for an umpire, whose vision is usually obscured by the batsman. In this case, even the eagle eyes of the television cameras could not give a clear indication. What was most disturbing was the behaviour of Bright. Despite his youth, at 23 he had been playing first-class cricket for six years and acceptance of the umpire's decision should have been automatic. His frustration was understandable in view of the general lack of success of the team but his actions were deserving of harsh condemnation.

The score was then 3/179. Greig and Boycott carried it to 201 shortly after tea, before Thomson got his faster delivery through the gap between Greig's bat and pad, spreadeagling his stumps, for 43. Boycott, on 81, was joined by Graham Roope, playing in his first Test match since 1975. With the packed crowd seething with anticipation, Boycott moved into the 90s, clipping Walker through mid-wicket for 2. Then it was 93, with a similar shot, signalling the end of Walker's day, in which he had sent down 26 overs for 55 runs without success, although often beating the bat.

Greg Chappell came on from the Members' Stand end.

138

Boycott moved to 95 with two singles from him, then pushed Pascoe to cover to reach 96. The great moment came in Chappell's next over. A half-volley was struck firmly past mid-on to the boundary: Boycott's 100th hundred in first-class cricket. Chappell barely had time to shake his hand, and Boycott to raise bat and hands triumphantly in the air when the milling hordes were on him. For several minutes, the focus of England's attention disappeared from view. When the hands of the constabulary had rescued him, Boycott was minus cap and still in a state of intense emotion. The ground clock showed history had been made at 5.50 p.m. on 11 August and those who were there are never likely to forget it.

The cold, hard facts were that it was Boycott's 14th Test century, his second in successive Tests since his comeback, his 100th century coming from 645 visits to the crease, in 324 minutes on this day with 14 fours. For the fanatical cricket-lovers of Yorkshire county, it was a magical moment, stressing to the world what was written on myriad T-shirts: that Boycott, indeed, could walk on water. Well, almost.

The Australians sat around for five minutes while order was restored, the youth who had souvenired the batsman's cap returned it, and a Test match continued. Somehow, the indefatigable Boycott retained his concentration and by stumps, was 110 not out, with Roope 19 and England a comfortable 4/252.

Over an excellent dinner of fish and chips that night, at the famed Brett's restaurant, Brearley confided that it was England's hope to bat forever in this game. A marathon occupation of the crease would ensure Australia could not win. And no Australian victory meant the Ashes for England.

Occupation was obviously to the forefront of Boycott's mind when play resumed under overcast skies the next morning. The Australian bowlers again underwent a succession of near misses as both batsmen, but especially Roope, played and missed to Walker and Thomson. It couldn't last forever, and in Thomson's fourth over of the morning, Roope caught a thick edge which Walters at third slip clutched gratefully. Knott came in at 5/275 and proceeded to play most sedately, scoring only four in his first 55 minutes. Bright was on after 90 minutes play and Knott immediately swept him for four. Boycott reached 145 as he leg-glanced Thomson to the boundary, his highest score against Australia, eclipsing his 142 not out at Sydney in the 1970–71 series. By lunch, England was impregnable at 5/339. Boycott had added only 39 in the two-hour session to be 149 with Knott 26.

Boycott reached his 150 straight after lunch, in 492 minutes with 19 fours, but it was not until 3.35 p.m. that Knott swept once too often at Bright and was adjudged lbw by Alley. His 57 had taken exactly three hours, with 7 fours. Three balls later, a surprised Botham played inside the line to Bright and lost his off-bail for a duck. Underwood helped to raise the 400, and was dropped by Chappell at slip off Bright, another easy chance that emphasized the decline in Australia's fielding standards. Underwood was eighth man out, victim of a great diving catch in the gully by Bright off Pascoe, but England was still in charge at tea, with Boycott grinding on inexorably to 179 out of a total of 8/418. Eighteen runs after the break, it was all over. First Pascoe had Hendrick caught at short leg by Robinson and then Boycott finally made a fatal mistake. He attempted to drive Pascoe, but gave Chappell an easy catch at slip instead. He was last man out, for 191 out of a total of 436, made in 10 hours and 28 minutes with 23 fours. It was an extraordinary effort of discipline and concentration, but because of its snail's pace probably would have been viewed with distaste anywhere but in front of his home crowd. On the first day, thousands had crowded in front of the players' pavilion to pay homage to Boycott and they were to repeat the salute again this night.

Pascoe limped off the field with the best Australian figures, 4/91 off 34.4 overs but his leg injuries had caught up with him and he was destined not to bowl another ball in anger on tour. Walker had been the best of the Australians, repeatedly beating the bat, yet finishing with 0/97 off 48 overs.

Australia began its saving operation at 5.05 p.m. when McCosker and Davis walked out to face Willis and Hendrick. Eighty-five minutes later, at stumps, the innings lay in tatters. The Ashes were lost—perhaps forever if the Packer fight got out of control—and the reputation of this team had reached its lowest ebb in a tour noted for its ever-deteriorating scale of performances. McCosker faced the first over from Willis and took eight runs in workmanlike fashion. Davis shaped up to Hendrick, went forward to the second delivery and Lloyd Budd hardly hesitated in declaring him lbw for 0.

Chappell came in, admittedly in failing light and with rain threatening, but hardly gave the impression of working for a long stay. To the first ball of Hendrick's third over, he pushed forward haphazardly and gave his rival leader an easy offering at first slip. Australia 2/26, then witnessed the largest stand of the innings: 26 between McCosker and Hookes. Both men seemed intent on scoring as quickly as possible, Hookes in particular was risking everything in his lust for runs. The situation hardly justified such tactics.

After posting the 50 in 47 minutes—27 minutes faster than England's equivalent—Hookes pushed defensively forward to Hendrick. For reasons best known to himself, McCosker backed up too far and the lightning reflexes of Randall moving across from extra-cover, enabled him to pick up and flick the ball into the stumps of the startled McCosker. Australia 3/52, last man run out 27.

The score advanced to 57 when Botham, with the third ball of his second over, had Hookes lbw for 24—playing across the line. Botham struck again in his fourth over when Walters edged an easy catch to Hendrick at third slip. Australia went in at stumps, 5/67, and in disgrace, to put it mildly. Its batsmen yet again had shown total disregard for the position, attempting all kinds of flamboyance against an attack that rarely wavered from the line and fieldsmen who sweated on every half-chance that came their way. It was a continual source of amazement to some cricket writers on this tour that the batsmen often tried to lessen their culpability with cries of 'hard luck' and 'bad decision'. When Hookes tried that tack in the team hotel that night, his voice was drowned out in a wave of scorn.

With rain threatening and the light poor, it was a surprise that play began on time on the third morning. It took Mike Hendrick and Ian Botham only 46 minutes to complete the rout of Australia for 103, its lowest total in a Test match on this famous old ground. Marsh and Robinson resumed for Australia but added only 10 runs before Marsh was out. The Australian vice-captain, unhappy owner of a pair in the previous Test, leg-glanced Botham finely and was somewhat amazed as Knott tumbled to his left and held the half-chance in an outstretched left glove. The disastrous position didn't alter Robinson's cavalier approach. He sent two deliveries from Hendrick crashing through the covers, tried for one more but sent it to second slip where Greig juggled then held the catch. From 7/87, Bright and Walker added 13 runs in seven minutes before Walker, aiming a big hit, edged to Knott off Botham. Thomson lasted only three balls before he was beaten and bowled by Botham and Pascoe completed the disgrace when he pushed forward to Hendrick only to find his stumps in disarray.

The innings had lasted only 132 minutes, and Australia was 333 runs behind with no chance of rescuing the Ashes. Botham and Hendrick had bowled superbly, it is true, but their analyses were helped immeasurably by batting that was indisputably well below Test or even first-class standard. Only three players, McCosker, Hookes and Robinson, had reached double figures and Botham, 5/21 off 11 overs, had taken five wickets in an innings in each of his first two Test matches.

Davis and McCosker began the humiliating follow-on just before 12.30 p.m. This side no longer made hope spring eternal in Australian hearts and if that was pessimism at its worst, it was also truth. Davis relished the introduction of Greig into the attack after seven overs, twice hitting him off the back foot for four, then producing a classical cover drive. When he glanced Greig, however, there was little Knott making ground to his left to make a difficult catch look easy. Australia was 1/31 and Knott had claimed his 250th victim in Test matches, the first man to do so. Once started, Australia's debacles rarely lost momentum and so it was to be. Only four more runs were added before McCosker, finding Greig a difficult proposition, edged him towards first slip where Knott, anticipating well, made his 251st Test dismissal.

Lunch was taken amid speculation about the weather. The rain held off long enough for Australia to sink deeper into the mire. Hookes and Chappell defended stoutly for a while against the persistence of Willis, Hendrick, Greig and Botham until the score reached 63. Then Hendrick drew Hookes forward and Umpire Budd agreed the batsman was lbw for 21, a decision that brought a look of horror from the victim.

Walters joined his captain, who was applying rigid concentration and a classically straight bat to combat the bowlers, operating in a greyness that made batting an onerous task. Freddy, as Walters is known to team-mates, was immediately flashing and missing to the pace bowlers and giving no one the impression that he was planning a long stay. For variety, the seldom-used Woolmer was introduced with his medium-pacers and collected Walters with the first ball of his second over. The batsman, on 15, pushed forward indecisively and there was no doubt about that lbw decision.

Chappell and a subdued Robinson grafted to tea, when the score was 4/114. There was to be no further progress by England on this third day. Only three balls were bowled after the interval before Messrs Alley and Budd finally took pity on the batsmen. One hundred and nine minutes later, at 6.28 p.m., the teams reappeared when just about everybody, including most in the press box, had gone home. Play was possible under an English Test rule which allows for an extra hour's play after 6.30 p.m., if more than an hour has been lost to the weather during the day. But the rain came again after five more runs were added and Australia finished a day of ignominy at 4/120, with Chappell 29 and Robinson 11.

Just about Australia's only victory of note in the summer of 1977 came the next day, at the Harrogate county ground near Leeds. The Harrogate committee had gone to great lengths to make sure that the clash between the two press teams was a success and they could be rightly proud of their efforts. The main attraction to the battery of television cameras was Kerry Packer who flew to Leeds from London by helicopter. Good batting performances by Ian Chappell, David Frith and the author were ignored as Packer, batting at number eight made 2 not out in a total of 8/220. The English side could muster only 147 in reply, the highlight of which was a sharp slips catch which Packer held off the bowling of David Lord. It was a

143

happier Australian dressing room than most, even allowing for the fact that Mr Packer had taken legal action against two of his team-mates.

Monday, 15 August—fourth day of the Fourth Test—dawned wet and windy and to the uninitiated there seemed little chance of play. Such are the vagaries of the English summer, however, that only 110 minutes were lost and the game resumed, albeit on a dampish outfield, at 2 p.m.

Chappell immediately cut Willis for 3, but after 28 minutes and 10 runs, the slaughter was on again. Chappell, 36 in three hours, tried to force Willis on the off-side, but got only an edge of the bat to the ball which flew, at waist height, into Greig's reliable clutch. Now half the Australian side was out for 130 and the end was in sight. Marsh chose this moment to find his best batting form of the tour. The chunky left-hander played the way his admirers know he can: shrewd choice of the right ball to hit, allied with watchful defence. He scored 26 of a partnership of 37 with Robinson before losing his fellow wicket-keeper, bowled by a Hendrick off-cutter for 20, a delivery to which he offered no shot.

Marsh was enjoying some luck—Roope at third slip dropped him off Hendrick at 16—but he made the most of it. He lost Bright, caught comfortably by Greig again as he flashed at Hendrick, with the score 7/179 but found a willing partner in Walker. The pair added 65 in 57 minutes for the eighth wicket as Marsh charged to his half-century in 80 minutes with 9 fours. Randall, in the outfield, was captivated by a lady with obvious gifts, and etched an appropriate message in the turf. Unfortunately for him, the etching was seen by chairman of England selectors Alec Bedser, who later issued a stern reprimand. This by-play didn't hinder the England charge to victory, as Walker's brave stand of 30 ended when Bob Willis took the new ball at 7/244. His third delivery uprooted Walker's middle stump and two balls later Thomson lost his off stump. The latter was Willis' 100th Test match wicket. Three runs later, Marsh, on 63, swung desperately at Hendrick and Randall ran from extra-cover to accept the catch that finally brought the Ashes back to England. The exultant fieldsman threw the ball high in the air and celebrated with a series of cart-wheels across the Headingley outfield.

Australia, all out for 248, had lost its third Test of the series by a conclusive innings and 85 runs. England was 3–0 up in a home series against Australia, for the first time since 1886, by dint of outplaying its opponents in every facet of the game for most of the series. Such a victory was not to be ignored by the Yorkshire fans, who crammed in their thousands to pay tribute to the England team. While champagne corks popped, the triumphant home team made curtain-call after curtain-call on the balcony. No one, of course, made as many as Geoff Boycott although Hendrick, with match figures of 8/95, was entitled to a great share of the adulation. The match had finished at 4.40 p.m. and just over an hour later, the crowd was still roaring for its heroes, so much so that the BBC television broadcasting team could hardly make itself heard above the hubbub.

About that time, Greg Chappell was telling a bevy of cricket writers that The Oval test match would be the last of his distinguished career. Chappell, generally conceded to be the best of Australia's post-war batsmen, was retiring, he said, for personal reasons. He had spent little time at his Brisbane home in the last few years. He was in England during the birth of his first son, Stephen, in 1975 and had left for this tour only nine days after the birth of his second child, a daughter, Belinda. The Australian captain had indicated at the start of this tour that it could well be his last. Now he would retire after 52 Tests in which he hit 4097 runs at the champion's average of 53.20. As well, he had taken 73 catches, mostly at slip, and 32 wickets with his medium pacers. There were two other reasons behind his decision. The knowledge that his health—he suffers from chronic bronchitis and has never fully recovered from an attack of glandular fever four years ago—did not help him stand the rigours put on Test cricketers today, and the prospect of earning good money in a short space of time as one of the Packer players. 'The Packer offer', he explained 'came at exactly the right time for me'. There was some speculation, too, that Chappell had retired before the Australian Cricket Board could make a ruling on the provident fund money it held for its Test players, in Chappell's case, more than $10,000.

145

There was no doubt that Chappell would leave the Test scene a bitterly disappointed man. The 1977 tourists had let him down in almost every conceivable way. Never the extrovert, he had tried to lead by example; in 1977, no one had been willing, or able, to follow the example. His captaincy record, on his retirement, read: played 17, won 8, lost 5, drawn 4. And five of those victories came in his first series, against the West Indies in the summer of 1974–75.

FOURTEEN

Now the tourists travelled back to London for the final stage of the arduous trip to England. No matter what the result of the series, Australian cricket authorities surely must realize that the old-fashioned full-length tours are out-moded. With players involved in Test cricket virtually the whole year— Australia played 12 Tests in 1977—shorter tours are a necessity. There must no longer be matches against all the counties; they should be contained to six or eight on a rota system and the Test matches scheduled closer together. As well, better facilities such as accommodation must be found, as undoubtedly they will in the wake of the Packer affair.

There was little incentive for the Australians to fight back, and they played the two lead-up games to the final Test that way. Most of us who travelled, for the second time this summer, to historic Arundel Castle had trouble with navigation. But it was no surprise to find Australia 5/20 against a richly-talented Rest of the World side in the one-day limited over game. Only Hookes and Chappell reached double figures in a total of 106 against Bob Willis, Imran Khan, Eddie Barlow, Mike Procter and Derek Underwood. Walker, Malone and Dymock all bowled well to make the composite side struggle for its three wicket victory. Malone's effort probably sealed his Fifth Test spot, as Pascoe was given little chance of recovering from his leg and groin injuries in time.

The last county fixture, against Middlesex at Lord's, was marred by rain, but hardly did anything to lift flagging morale. After dismissing the county champions for a modest 207, the Australians crashed against the astonishing pace of West Indian Wayne Daniel who claimed 4/27 as the side crumbled

147

for 149, its second lowest first-class total of the entire tour. Daniel, who had signed with the Packer troupe, gave a taste of things to come when he dismissed Marsh and Walters with deliveries that brought inelegant reactions from the batsmen.

Despite the contention of many English cricket writers that the Packer rebels Knott, Greig and Underwood would be omitted from the England team, now the Ashes had been recovered, the selectors retained the same 12 for the Fifth Test. Ian Botham subsequently withdrew when it was found he had a broken bone in his foot, an injury that was to rob him of the chance to achieve the coveted double of 1000 runs and 100 wickets in a county season.

Beside the cricket, there were more moves in the Packer drama. An angry Max Walker denied a Melbourne report that said he, too, was retiring from Test cricket. 'I am committed to Mr Packer. If that means I am banned from Test cricket, that is too bad. But I am definitely not retiring', Walker emphasized.

Mr Packer himself, in an interview published in the London *Sunday Telegraph* on 21 August, said he was still prepared to go back to talks with the International Cricket Conference at any time. 'There is still time for compromise', he insisted.

The Packer organization then announced it would play its matches in Sydney at the Showground and in Perth at the Gloucester Park Trotting track. It was pointed out, however, that if the Sydney Cricket Ground became available, as it subsequently did, Packer had the right to withdraw from the Showground venue.

And in England, Packer troupe member Mushtaq Mohammed resigned the captaincy of Northamptonshire because of doubt about his future with the county, for which he had been playing since 1964.

The Oval authorities were reporting yet another sellout of Test match tickets, despite the state of the series. Not surprisingly, the three Australian selectors were in as big a quandary about their Fifth Test team, as they had been in April when a squad of untried, largely inexperienced cricketers stepped off the jet at Heathrow. Eventually, they settled on a squad of 13, including Mick Malone and Kim Hughes for the first time, and reinstating Craig Serjeant who had missed the last two Tests. It was almost only an academic exercise as heavy rain had fallen in London for five days preceding the Test and on the Wednesday, The Oval surface was awash. But Davis and Robinson had at last been discarded from the squad and Pascoe, it was known, would not play in spite of his determination to prove his fitness. In fact, the side could have done with a large injection of the Pascoe spirit.

Umpires Tom Spencer and David Constant made only two cursory inspections of the ground before deciding at 2.30 p.m. that there would be no play on the first day. Indeed, there was some surprise when play was able to start on time on the second. Chappell won the toss for third time in the series and decided England should bat, after the Australians had left O'Keeffe out of the squad and made Pascoe 12th man, thus giving Western Australians Hughes and Malone belated debuts in Test cricket. England caused no surprise by naming Miller 12th man for his second successive Test. With piles of sawdust surrounding the wicket area, Thomson and Malone began proceedings to Brearley and Boycott. The last ball of Malone's first over shaved Boycott's bat and dropped just short of Chappell at slip. The tall ex-Subiaco ruckman was able to move the ball late in the heavy conditions and both batsmen had to defend watchfully.

The Test seemed to be going along the same path as its predecessors, however, when McCosker at slip put down a straightforward chance from Brearley when that man was 19 and the score 42. Not only was it another inexcusable fielding lapse, but it robbed Malone of his maiden Test wicket. He was to make up for the disappointment before the day was out. The 50 took an inordinately long time, 99 minutes and 25 overs, but the bowling had been tight and the outfield slow. When Bright relieved Malone from the Vauxhall end, the opener had sent down 13 overs, and conceded only 15 runs. It was to be his only respite for the day. England, 0/60 at lunch, appeared to have overcome its starting problems. The score climbed to 86 just before 3 o'clock when Walker's inswinger caught the inside edge of Boycott's bat and the ball rebounded from his pad into the air and McCosker at last caught something worthwhile. Boycott's 39 runs had come from a stay of 171 minutes and for

149

once he would not dog the Australians for a long time. At Trent Bridge, he had batted for all but 105 minutes of England's time while at Leeds he had been at the crease for the entire innings.

Now Malone proceeded to take advantage of the break-through. Eight balls after Boycott's demise, he induced Brearley to stab at an outswinger which a tumbling Marsh caught triumphantly in his right hand. Brearley was on his way to the pavilion for 39, with England 2/88 and Malone was on his way to a sensational debut. A strangely indecisive Randall helped Woolmer to take the total past 100, in 211 minutes, then he became another victim of the Marsh-Malone combination. The outswinger took a fine edge and the wicketkeeper picked up the chance low and to the right. That gave Malone 2/36 off 26.4 overs. Thomson, in the next over, trapped Woolmer lbw for 15, as he played forward, then Malone had Greig caught in the gully for 0, from the first ball of his next over. England, 5/106, was now in trouble; even the Australian fielding had become sharp.

Knott wasn't the man to save the situation this time. He made only six before he prodded forward to Malone and McCosker scooped up the low catch at second slip. Umpire Tom Spencer was in some doubt as to the validity of the catch but Knott saved him the trouble of conferring with David Constant, by departing in an act of good sportsmanship. England slumped further when Malone trapped Lever lbw for 3 with one that came back off the seam. Of a total of 7/130, Malone had 5/40 from a marathon 34.3 overs.

Roope, missed off a difficult caught and bowled chance by Malone when 11, got some valuable help from Underwood in an attempt to right the innings. The pair added 39. There was no rest for Malone who took the new ball with Thomson at 7/169. But it was Thomson's turn now and with his third delivery, he scattered Roope's stumps as he played inside the line. That was Thomson's 21st wicket for the series and his 100th in Tests, a remarkable effort for a man written off as an athlete last Christmas Eve. The night before, he had been voted Australia's bowler of the series by the Victoria Sporting club in London, an award worth 500 jubilee crowns ($200). Similar awards had gone to Greg Chappell, and Geoff Boycott and

Bob Willis for England. Thomson repeated the treatment to Underwood with the first delivery of his second over with the new ball and England was near the end at 9/174. Mike Hendrick and Willis resisted until stumps when the score was 9/181.

The sum of Malone's work for the day was 43 overs, 20 maidens, 53 runs and 5 wickets. Remarkable figures in any bowlers' language, they were all the more commendable when it was realized that this was the first time he had bowled in a Test match, and he had had remarkable little bowling during the tour to fit him for such an assignment. To those of us who had been disappointed with team selections during the series, the question immediately arose: what would have happened if he had been given a chance earlier?

Perhaps it was only fitting that the weather, which had given the Australians such a miserable start to the tour, should intervene again to wipe out any chance of ending it on a victorious note. Only 77 minutes of play was made available by the elements before Umpires Spencer and Constant called off play for the day, in what looked like the start of the Arctic winter.

In that time, England had made some ground after its worst start of the series the day previous. Hendrick and Willis had swung the bat so effectively when play resumed 10 minutes late because of bad light and rain, that they extended their last wicket stand to 40. Willis, in fact, brought up the 200 when he cover-drove Malone for four, the first boundary from the lanky Western Australian's bowling. After 43 minutes, Hendrick finally stepped away from his stumps once too often and Thomson knocked his off stump out of the ground.

Rain was falling on the pitch as the players left the arena with England's first innings standing at 214. It delayed the start of Australia's innings by 10 minutes and when play was possible again, Serjeant came out to open the innings with McCosker. The light rain helped Willis to skid the ball through and with the last ball of his first over, found Serjeant's pads in front of his stumps as he failed to commit himself to a defensive stroke. So Chappell marched onto The Oval for his last Test innings in familiar position: 1/0. At lunch, it was 1/6 and bad light held up play for another 80 minutes. Then Willis bowled one more over, which yielded five runs before the rain came teeming down with Australia 1/11. Play was finally abandoned for the day at 4.30 p.m.

Best news of the day—for England cricketers anyway— came with the announcement of a $1.6 million sponsorship from the giant insurance company Cornhill. Cornhill general manager Mr Cecil Burrows said the money would be injected into cricket over five years, with the possibility of more to follow. Final details had not been worked out, but one point had been agreed. Players representing England in Test matches would receive at least $1600 per player per match. More money would be available for overseas tours and there was provision for money to be channelled to the counties, the minor counties and the National Cricket Association, which controls junior cricket in the United Kingdom. The sponsorship deal, the largest yet in the sport, was a result of the efforts of businessman David Evans, who had set up sponsorship of the England team for the last two Tests and who had appealed to business houses for sponsorship to offset the big money lure of the Packer contracts.

Bright sun and a drying wind on the rest day enabled play to start on time on the fourth day, although almost all chance of a result had been ruined. Almost immediately, McCosker had a life when Hendrick at third slip put down a difficult chance in Willis' second over of the day. Chappell was in an aggressive mood, unleashing some classical shots and some streaky ones as the pair added 28 runs in the first 35 minutes. The captain's, and the crowd's, hopes for a farewell century were not to be, however. After posting the 50 in 102 minutes, Chappell, on 39, skipped down the wicket to Underwood, but his half-drive was uppish and Underwood made no mistake with the return catch. Chappell's final innings had occupied 113 minutes and included 3 fours.

The curly-headed Kim Hughes, in his debut, had an uncomfortable time facing Underwood, who was bowling expertly and extracting some turn. It took Hughes 47 minutes and 33 deliveries to gain his first run—a push to extra cover off Hendrick, soon after lunch. But Hendrick had his revenge quickly when a ball moved away late, took the edge of Hughes' bat and carried swiftly to Willis at third slip. Australia, at 3/67 was faring no better than its opponent. The position had hardly improved when the patient McCosker was fourth man out at 84. After 201 minutes of defence and 32 runs, he tried to turn Willis on the on-side, but was lbw to a delivery which kept mysteriously low. Hookes, in the meantime, had begun his innings with a series of boundary shots, looking more like the player whose advance publicity in England had made him out to be another champion. At 104, he lost Walters, certainly playing his last Test in England. Walters was completely beaten and bowled by a Willis delivery that dipped in late. He walked slowly from the ground, still without a century after 18 Tests in England.

The left-handers Hookes and Marsh proceeded to rescue the side with a sixth wicket stand of 80 in 109 minutes. Marsh, finally finding some form with the bat after a dismal series, was content to let his younger partner be the aggressor. Hookes reached his half-century in 100 minutes with 6 fours and Australia at tea was 5/143. After the break, Hookes opened out, driving the fast bowlers with ease and advancing to within sight of his first Test century. Shrewdly, Brearley introduced Greig into the attack and Hookes, in trying to drive his old foe, edged an easy catch to Knott. His 85 had taken 154 minutes and included 12 fours.

Now Marsh took over the aggressor's role as Bright was content to defend. He drove Hendrick for successive fours and reached his half-century in the last over before stumps, hooking Willis for four. A few minutes earlier, he had swung Underwood over the long-on fence for six. By stumps, Australia had reached a narrow lead of 12, being 6/226 with Marsh 53 and Bright 6.

The last day of the series began with no chance of a result. Marsh was soon out, unhappily lbw to Hendrick after adding four to his overnight total. Bright followed him quickly, lbw to Willis for 16. Then came a remarkable ninth wicket stand of 100 between Walker and Malone. Both players recorded their highest figures in first-class cricket, Walker being left with 78 not out and Malone 46. Both had their share of good fortune—

Walker was missed at 9 and 19 and Malone before he had scored. But each used his massive reach to strike the fast bowlers into vacant spaces and each ran intelligently between wickets. Walker took 94 minutes to reach his inaugural Test half-century, with 6 fours and in all batted 2 hours and 7 minutes with 10 fours. Malone was at the wicket for 105 minutes for 6 fours, before he finally lost his leg-stump trying to turn Lever on the leg-side.

Thomson gave Walker willing support for a last wicket stand of 33, before he presented Willis with his 27th wicket of the series as he tried a big drive. Australia, all out for 385, led by 171. It was the tourists' highest score of the series, and the Walker-Malone stand the second highest behind the 104 runs Walters and Serjeant added in the Jubilee Test at Lord's.

In spite of the Australians' last-ditch bid for victory, time and the weather had run out on them. England began its second innings at 2.45 p.m. on the last day. Thomson had Brearley caught at short-leg for 4, in his third over and Malone had Woolmer caught by Marsh in his fourth over. England was 2/16 but didn't lose another wicket before bad light stopped play at 4.50 p.m., 70 minutes early. Boycott was 25 not out and Randall on 20 in a total of 2/57.

So the 1977 Ashes series was over with England decisive 3-0 winners. The only credit the Australians could take was for their efforts in the First and Fifth Tests. For the rest, England, with a finely balanced line-up and excellent fielding, was much the stronger. The Test averages showed this. Geoff Boycott, who played in only three games, towered over the batsmen with 442 from five innings at the massive average of 147.33, well ahead of Bob Woolmer, 394 runs at 56.28. But England had four other batsmen, Knott, Roope, Randall and Greig who all averaged better than 30 for every appearance at the crease.

Australia's leading batsman, on figures, was spin bowler Kerry O'Keeffe, who scored only 125 runs from 6 innings, 4 not outs, for an average of 62.5. Greg Chappell was the only Australian to score over 300 runs—371 at 41.22, and David Hookes the only other tourist to average better than 30—31.44. The remainder of the Australian batsmen can be ranked as failures; only twice did Australians hit Test centuries: Chappell at Old Trafford and McCosker at Trent Bridge. Australia lost both games. Five times English batsmen managed three figures: Boycott (2), Woolmer (2) and Knott.

England also held a decisive edge in fast bowling where the outstanding player was Bob Willis with 27 wickets at 19.77. Ian Botham (10), Mike Hendrick (14), Derek Underwood (13) and Tony Greig (7) all averaged less than 30 runs a wicket. Apart from Malone, who took 6 wickets at 12.8 in his only appearance, Australia's main striking force was Thomson with 23 wickets at 25.34. Pascoe captured 13 wickets at 27.92, Bright 5 at 29.40 and the unlucky Walker, 14 at 39.35.

Perhaps the most telling factor was the catching. Australia put down 17 chances during the series, many of them from batsmen who went on to make significant contributions. England, on the other hand, missed 8 but the first of these did not come until the second innings of the Fourth Test, when the game was already won.

Early in the tour, after the MCC game at Lord's, former England all-rounder Trevor Bailey had been moved to write in the *Financial Times* that this was the weakest Australian side on record. He came under heavy fire at the time. By the end of August, he could count himself a good judge.

FIFTEEN

The existence of the Packer troupe of professional cricketers has caused the greatest furore in cricket history. Of that statement, there is no dispute. But the exact origins of the idea of the troupe are obscure, even to people in the Packer organization. One version of the origin is that it was suggested to Kerry Packer several years ago by Mr Bruce Gyngell, who was then a highly-paid consultant to the Channel Nine Network. At that time, Packer was examining the possibility of moving into the televising and sponsoring of sport in a way never before attempted in Australia. The story widely accepted by the Australian cricketers now involved in the troupe is that Dennis Lillee suggested it, in a casual conversation to television personality and entrepreneur John Cornell in the winter of 1976. Cornell took the idea to Mr Packer, who, after some thought, came up with the idea of signing the world's top cricketers to play in a series of televised games for amounts of money that they had never dreamed they would be able to command.

This was the story that was abroad in cricket circles in September of 1976. On 2 October 1976, I wrote in the *Age*, Melbourne: 'Some of Australia's leading cricketers have been offered lucrative contracts to become part of an interstate cricket troupe. The plan could lead to a major confrontation between the players and the Australian Cricket Board. Under the plan, top cricketers could earn up to $30,000 each in a season, appearing in matches and promotions as a troupe of professional cricketers.' The story went on to say that the plan had been devised by executives of Channel 9.

Mr Packer is chairman of directors of Australian Consolidated Press, whose publication the *Bulletin*, in its detailed story of the Packer troupe on 14 May, claimed the saga began in November 1976. Then Cornell, and an old friend, journalist Austin Robertson, decided to form J.P. Sport to act as an agent for sporting personalities, including cricketers Rod Marsh, Dennis Lillee and David Hookes. According to the *Bulletin*, a couple of Australia's top cricketers asked Cornell and Robertson to do something for cricket. The troupe, or 'circus', developed rapidly from there, said the *Bulletin*.

Mr Packer himself has given a quite different side to the story. In an interview in early August with reporters from the London *Sunday Times*, some of which is reproduced here with permission, Packer said he did not begin the idea of an international troupe of cricketers playing super matches until he had been frustrated three times in efforts to get cricket television rights for Channel 9.

In the interview, Mr Packer said he had been ready to make his first bid to the Australian Cricket Board early in 1976. 'I feel it was the old boys' network', said Mr Packer. 'They offered me the commercial rights, but they said they would not sell the non-commercial rights away from the Australian Broadcasting Commission in any circumstances and at the time I hadn't even made a bid. I was simply outknifed.

'I said to Parish [Bob Parish, chairman of the Australian Cricket Board]: "I am prepared to pay half a million dollars a year for the rights when the ABC TV contract runs out in three years." Parish went white. I think the ABC had paid $50,000. I said I would sign the contract there and then. But I never heard back on that offer.'

Mr Packer decided to try again last summer to bid against the ABC for the rights to the 1977 Ashes series in England. 'News of my secret negotiations was leaked back to ABC TV in Australia so that they could get together a counter-bid. That was knife number two', he said.

'I told one of my blokes to go to London, put $240,000 (£150,000 sterling) down on the desk and tell them they have got 24 hours. Now that was $120,000 (£75,000 sterling) more than they were going to get. I wanted the counties in England to be so upset with the Test and County Cricket Board if they knocked back $240,000 (£75,000) and got only $120,000 (£75,000). I wanted them to ask: why didn't they get the top price?'

Mr Packer said that his winning of the TCCB contract led immediately to the ACB's insistence that in future only they would have the right to negotiate TV contracts for any Test cricket involving Australia outside Australia. In Mr Packer's eyes, that effectively shut him out of televising cricket. 'What chance have I of getting the rights now?' he asked. 'None.'

Mr Packer said that by shutting him out of any future bidding, the ACB drove him to activate his super match plan. 'That's when it happened', said Mr Packer. 'Three times the stiletto went in, and at the end of the third time, I said "that's it". That's how super test was born.' He said it was then— February 1977—that Cornell came to him.

Mr Packer was asked how much the players would benefit from the troupe, particularly after their three-year contracts ran out. 'If the players are good enough', he said bluntly 'they will be re-signed. If not, they won't be.'

Asked whether the Packer plan can really benefit cricket as it is run today, he said: 'The question is whether people with money are going to be allowed into sport. I think that the cricket boards are suffering from a self-inflicted wound—they got up with a shotgun and decided to blow their own toes off'.

During the interview, made just after the Third Test, Mr Packer claimed his network had not lost one ball of the series because of commercials. He added that the ratings for the first three Tests of the 1977 series showed that they had been 'an enormous programming success'. The ratings I have seen showed that the 1977 series rated best in Adelaide, followed by Melbourne and Sydney, where they just about broke even with the other two commercial channels. Strangely, the Third and Fourth Tests rated better in all three cities than did the first two.

The Australian Cricket Board had been strangely quiet on the subject of the Packer drama, ever since the story broke on 9 May. In fact, the Board had made only one brief statement on 11 May, reiterating that it was the sole organizing body for recognized cricket in this country. Nothing more was said until

158

Board chairman, Mr Bob Parish, released a long statement after the ACB meeting in Sydney on 7 September. The statement refuted many of the contentions made by Mr Packer and his organization during the past four months and detailed payments to Australian cricketers and other points at issue.

On the topic of payments to Australian players, Mr Parish said: 'The Board resolved in 1974 that it would pay to the players the maximum it could afford taking into consideration its overall responsibility to Australian cricket at all other levels. This principle was unanimously accepted by the State captains Greg Chappell, Doug Walters, Richie Robinson, Ashley Woodcock and Rod Marsh at the inaugural meeting of the Board Cricket sub-committee on 22 December 1976. The Board is of the opinion that it is honouring this undertaking and that Australian players are well paid.' The statement then quoted a passage from the recently-published Greg Chappell book *The 100th Summer* in which the then Australian captain said, 'Cricketers rewards have increased dramatically in a comparatively short time ... It's hardly surprising that Australia leads the way in providing a far better deal for cricketers.'

Mr Parish then detailed payments to Australian Test players: 'If a player played in two Pakistan Tests, for which he received $2481, toured New Zealand, played in the Centenary Test, toured the UK and was selected to play in the first two Tests against India, for which he would receive $3704, he would receive from the Board in the calendar year, 1977, nearly $22,000. In addition to that amount, the players receive match fees, prize money and sponsorship fees from Sheffield Shield and Gillette Cup matches and the Board pays all travel and accommodation costs plus meal allowances, both at home and abroad.'

Mr Parish said the ACB would allocate 30 per cent of the Benson and Hedges sponsorship of first-class cricket over the next two years to the players as prize money. These amounted to $75,000 for the 1977–78 season and $105,000 in 1978–79.

Mr Parish continued: 'Under the Benson and Hedges "team" sponsorship, the amount paid by the Board to each player will be $802 for each Test against India. Prize money for each Test will be $9,000—$6,000 ($500 each) to the winners and $3,000 ($250 each) to the losers. There will be Man of the Match awards of $500 for each Test. So each player, including the 12th man, in each Test will receive from the Board for five days cricket a minimum of $1852 and a maximum of $2102 depending on whether the match is won or lost.

On the questions of television, Mr Parish said:

It has been reported that the Board has denied television rights to the Channel 9 Network. In late March 1976, a representative of the 9 Network telephoned the secretary of the Board and advised him that the Network was interested in cricket television rights. No mention was made of total exclusivity and the Board took this to mean commercial rights which customarily had been negotiated with interested commercial stations after a contract with the ABC had been concluded. On 6 May, the Board television sub-committee commenced negotiations with the ABC. At this meeting and following subsequent negotiations, agreement was reached with the ABC on the usual non-exclusive basis for a three-year period concluding at the end of the 1978–79 season. Following normal procedure, all commercial television networks were advised of this agreement by letter dated 11 June.

On 22 June, the Board television sub-committee met representatives of the Television Corporation Ltd, who, at that meeting made a verbal offer for total exclusive rights for five years. Television Corporation representatives were informed that in view of the Board's agreement with the ABC, it was not possible for the sub-committee to consider the offer. The sub-committee was then asked whether it would be prepared to recommend to the Board acceptance of the offer to operate from the conclusion of the ABC contract.

The sub-committee was not prepared to make such a recommendation as the Board had never in the history of its television negotiations granted total exclusivity to any network. It was agreed that the 9 Network's interest in total exclusivity of Australian cricket television would be reported to the full Board at its September meeting. The verbal offer was thereupon withdrawn.

Subsequently the Board received two letters from the Executive vice-president of GTV Pty Ltd, Melbourne, dated

27 and 31 August. The first letter advised the Board that a proposition would be submitted on behalf of Consolidated Press and the National Nine Network. The second letter advised that it would not be possible to submit the proposal in time for the Board meeting to be held in Brisbane on 8, 9 and 10 September.

The Board received both these letters at its September meeting and a report from the television sub-committee in regard to the meeting held in Melbourne on 22 June. On 8 November, the Board secretary wrote to GTV 9 Melbourne acknowledging the two letters and advising that the Board was prepared to consider any written proposal for the televising of cricket that the Channel 9 Network cared to submit.

The Board has received no reply to this letter.

Finally, the Australian Board was consulted by the U.K. Test and County Cricket Board in early February 1977 regarding negotiations taking place concerning the relay to Australia of the just concluded England–Australia Test series. The Board was informed that a substantial offer had been received from the 9 Network. The Board expressed the view that any decision concerning this offer was the prerogative of the English authorities but the Board hoped, in view of the support that cricket had received from the ABC over the years and the fact that the ABC could give national coverage, that it would be possible to make some joint arrangement and the ABC would not be totally excluded.

The Board firmly believes that it has acted properly in these matters. Other than the verbal offer made to the television sub-committee on 22 June 1976, no offer or proposal from the 9 Network for exclusive television rights of Australian cricket has been received by the Board.

SIXTEEN

The Australian tourists began drifting home, or for holidays, almost as soon as the Fifth Test had finished. Many of them had been joined by their wives at different stages of the tour; now they took the opportunity to visit Europe or America before returning to prepare for a domestic season that promised to be interesting in the extreme, if not sensational.

The old, old debate of whether wives should be allowed to accompany their husbands on tour had continued almost right through the 1977 series. At least four of the Australians had linked up with their spouses as early as May; team officials turned virtually a blind eye, demanding only that the players be present at team meetings, matches and official functions. At one stage, just before the last Test, nine of the players had their wives in England. There had been harsh words spoken between some of the players at Leeds during the Fourth Test: those who believed that all members of the team should be together, socially as well as on the field, for the sake of team spirit and harmony, and others who argued that wives and loved ones had a settling effect on players on tour. I tend to believe the former. Yet the refusal of cricket authorities in the past to allow wives on tour without special permission was brought up by Tony Greig as an argument in favour of the Packer plan, during the High Court trial in London in late September. Australia's last two captains—Ian Chappell and Greg Chappell—are both firm believers that wives should not accompany their husbands on tour. I believe that in 1977 the presence of wives did not help the Australians. There was one case of a player making himself unavailable for a county game because his wife didn't want him to play.

162

If the tourists thought they were returning home to peace and tranquillity, they were soon to be disillusioned. At least one of them, South Australian David Hookes, was deep in doubt over his decision to join the Packer troupe; on his return to Adelaide, he had long talks with officials on both sides of the fence, including South Australia Cricket Association president and Australian selector Phil Ridings. Hookes was offered long-term business prospects if he stayed on as a South Australian cricketer. On 1 October, the young left-hander announced he was going to spend a few days 'thinking over everything before making a decision'. He stayed with the troupe.

England selectors, sitting down to pick their touring side to Pakistan and New Zealand in the southern summer, got a couple of shocks too. On 3 September, batsman Bob Woolmer, one of the stars of the series against Australia, announced he was unavailable for the tour because of business and personal reasons. Later in the day, he revealed he had signed a three-year contract with the Packer troupe. It was also known that fast bowlers Bob Willis and Chris Old had been approached to join by Tony Greig. In the High Court, three weeks later, Greig was to deny that he had acted as Mr Packer's agent. He was paid a consultancy fee, Greig said, to explain to players just what the troupe was all about, and what it planned to achieve. Both Willis and Old were included in the England touring team. On 10 September, Old announced he had turned down the offer. 'I told Greig I wasn't interested', he said. On 26 September, the secretary of Willis' county club, Warwickshire, Mr Alan Smith, announced that Willis would be making the Pakistan-New Zealand tour. The much-improved England spearhead had resisted, temporarily at least, the Packer offer.

Len Maddocks, team manager of the Australians, arrived back in Sydney and stated emphatically that the furore over the Packer troupe had had 'a disastrous effect on team morale'. He was right, of course. Despite all the denials of Greg Chappell during the tour, the Packer business had weighed heavily on the minds of all the Australians. They would have been less than human if it hadn't.

The Australian Cricket Board met in Sydney on 6 and 7 September; it wasn't hard to guess what was the number one

163

topic on the agenda. Harsh reactions were expected from Australia's cricket administrators. At the end of the meeting, however, Board chairman Bob Parish announced that there would be no official ban on Packer players competing in Australian cricket. The matter, said Mr Parish, was still the subject of legal proceedings in Britain. He said the ACB was considering placing all first-class cricketers in the country under contract before they played matches. Although the wording of his statement was soft, it did mean that Packer players would be virtually unable to fulfil the Board demands because of their contracts with J.P. Sport Pty Ltd, now known as World Series Cricket.

On 5 October, Board secretary Alan Barnes said that the five states had agreed on a formula to operate between the states and players selected for Australian or State matches. Mr Barnes said players chosen would be required to complete a form, if they accepted the invitations to play. Mr Parish said copies of the contracts would be made available to players to give them a chance to study their implications. He repeated that the ACB was not banning players, but that they would have to make a decision for whom they played.

In England, a month earlier, an extraordinary meeting of the Players' Association called on Mr Packer to reschedule the dates for his proposed matches in Australia over the summer. One hundred and eighty members met in Birmingham on 5 September and heard Tony Greig put the case for the Packer troupe members. Then they voted 91-77 in favour of a motion calling on the TCCB and the ICC to re-open talks aimed at a compromise. They made this conditional on Mr Packer altering his playing dates, so they did not clash with the Australia–India Test matches. The meeting voted heavily in favour—139–36—of the ban on county players involved in the troupe.

Greig, who had spoken for 25 minutes, was not happy with the vote. 'We have all wasted our time; the motions are contradictory', he told Association secretary Jack Bannister, and president John Arlott after the meeting. The anti-Packer faction in the meeting was led by former England captain Ray Illingworth and Warwickshire batsman John Whitehouse.

In Australia, the moves were coming thick and fast. Richie Robinson defended his decision to join the troupe with the words: 'I know people say we have no loyalty, but loyalty won't get my sons a good education. That takes money and Packer was offering it at the right time'.

Those planning to watch the Packer games at VFL Park, Melbourne and Football Park, Adelaide discovered it was going to be an expensive outing. $6 a day would be the asking price at both venues. Outer seats cost $2 during the Centenary Test in Melbourne in March and the normal cost of a seat for a Test match at the Adelaide Oval is $3.

On 12 September, the Victorian Cricket Association became the first of the State bodies to lay down its policy on Packer players. It said it would leave a final decision to individual clubs on whether Packer players could take part in District (or club) matches. Permission, it indicated, was highly unlikely. The next day, Victorian selectors left the three players involved— Max Walker, Ray Bright and Richie Robinson—out of the State practice squad.

A similar line was taken in New South Wales, where the six Packer men were told that they would have to apply to the NSWCA for permission to play grade cricket. The Association also invoked an old by-law preventing players who have signed with an outside promoter from playing club cricket. On 4 October, the six—Doug Walters, Rick McCosker, Kerry O'Keeffe, Ian Davis, Len Pascoe and Gary Gilmour—were omitted from the State practice squad although Association secretary Bob Radford said: 'The State selectors were given no direction by the Association and are not required to give any reasons for their selection or non-selection of any player'.

Ian Chappell became the first of the Packer players to be excluded from club cricket when North Melbourne reluctantly told him that he could not play for them. Melbourne followed suit by sacking Walker as captain and a player. Footscray and Essendon then told Bright and Robinson respectively that their services were no longer required. South Melbourne and Ian Redpath parted company after an association lasting nearly 20 years.

The Western Australian Cricket Association council went

even further on 25 September when it banned Dennis Lillee, Rod Marsh, Mick Malone, Ross Edwards and a new Packer signatory, opening batsman Bruce Laird, from practising or playing with their clubs or the State squad.

Four days later, Lillee defied the ban by practising with Melville club. 'I'm employed by Melville as coach and I don't intend to stop coaching', he said after batting and bowling at the nets. Lillee took his action with the full support of the Melville committee, which faced only a $5 fine for its action, although the WACA promised the fine would be increased substantially in the future. Lillee, upset at the Association's action, advised any player selected for the Packer troupe to seize his opportunity. He also predicted a resolution to the conflict within a year. 'There has got to be a solution eventually. We can't go on fighting and carrying on like this', he said.

Western Australian Test batsmen Kim Hughes announced on 28 September that he had turned down an offer to join the troupe and urged other WA players to concentrate their thoughts on retaining the Sheffield Shield and representing Australia. And former Test batsman Ross Edwards, who was coming out of retirement to play for Mr Packer, hit out strongly at the WACA ban. 'The ban was the Association's ultimate weapon. They have now played their last card, but we haven't started to play our cards yet. From now on, the cricket establishment could be in for a few shocks.' Edwards was speaking en route to London to give evidence in the High Court case brought by J.P. Sport Pty Ltd, against the Test and County Cricket Board and the International Cricket Conference.

Those Packer players banned from club and State cricket immediately made plans to play minor grade cricket with non-affiliated associations in their respective States.

In South Australia, Hookes was allowed to play club cricket and to practise with the State squad, in which he had been chosen before he returned from England. Another allowed to play club cricket was spinner Ashley Mallett, who came out of retirement in September to sign for the troupe. In Brisbane, Greg Chappell, and Martin Kent were allowed to continue with their clubs. Later all four were banned.

166

Jeff Thomson's employer, radio station 4 IP, claimed in September that the fast bowler was being 'harassed' by representatives of the Packer organization. 'Jeff told us he wished to be left alone to play cricket for Queensland and Australia. As a result, we pointed out quietly but firmly that if the Packer people wish to speak to him, they should talk to us. In other words, we said "leave him alone"', said 4 IP lawyer Frank Gardiner.

On 20 September, World Series Cricket named a five-man governing committee to oversee the running of the troupe and its matches. Three former Test players, Richie Benaud, Bob Cowper and John Gleeson were on the committee with chairman Brian Treasure, the administrative controller of World Series Cricket and Geoff Forsaith, a former grade cricketer in Sydney and Perth. Ian Chappell was one of two players' representatives on the committee, the second was to be chosen after all overseas players assembled in Australia late in November.

Ian Chappell was also the moving force behind the first bid to establish an Australian Players' Association. At a meeting in Adelaide on 18 September, a working committee involving Chappell, Walker, Edwards and Queenslander John Maclean was formed. Chappell wanted the association to include both Packer and non-Packer players. Its future would lie in the reaction of players throughout the country, who were to be approached about joining in the next few months.

And on 26 September, in London's High Court, before Mr Justice Slade began the hearing that many thought could determine the future of the Packer cricket revolution. It was the much-publicized trial between J.P. Sport (now known as World Series Cricket), the TCCB and the ICC, and players Tony Greig, John Snow and Mike Procter. The players and J.P. Sport sought orders preventing the TCCB and the ICC banning Packer players from Test and county cricket.

The embattled parties each had a victory on 30 September. Then the new Sydney Cricket Ground Trust reversed its earlier decision and gave Mr Packer permission to play his matches there. It was a significant breakthrough for the rebel troupe. Now two five-day international matches and three one-day

167

games would be played on one of the recognized homes of the game in Australia. The news was released by Trust chairman, Mr Pat Hills, who also holds the Cabinet post of New South Wales Minister for Industrial Relations. The previous Trust had refused Mr Packer's application for the ground on 25 July and had been sacked by the State Government on 27 July. When the 13 new members were appointed, Mr Packer had made another application which was successful. Mr Hills refused to reveal the money that would be paid for the hire of the ground, but said it was 'a substantial bid'.

Not far away, in the Federal Court, Mr Packer's company, World Series Cricket, was ordered not to use the words 'Test' or 'Supertest' to describe their matches during the summer. The court decision also prevented the use of several planned television and press advertisements. It meant the ads, to be used by the Packer television network as part payment to World Series Cricket for the right to televise the games, would have to be remade. The company was restrained from 'any conduct that is misleading or deceptive or is likely to mislead or deceive'. The Court order was made on the application of Australian Cricket Board chairman, Mr Bob Parish, who claimed in his action, begun a week earlier, that promotion for Mr Packer's cricket matches inferred the Board was involved with or had approved them. The action followed an advertisement in the Australian *Women's Weekly*, two weeks earlier. The magazine, published by a Packer company, had used photographs of several players, including Ian Chappell, Alan Knott, Rod Marsh and Dennis Lillee. Marsh was among others wearing a cap with the insignia of the Australian team.

The next day, 1 October, the West Indies and Pakistan Boards of control announced that its players involved with Packer were now banned from Test cricket, in line with the ICC ultimatum. The West Indians were Clive Lloyd, Bernard Julien, Roy Fredericks, Gordon Greenidge, Andy Roberts, Michael Holdings, Collis King, Joel Garner, Deryck Murray, Laurence Rowe, Albert Padmore, David Holford, Viv Richards and Wayne Daniel. The five Pakistanis were Asif Iqbal, Mushtaq Mohammed, Imran Khan, Majid Khan and Zaheer Abbas.

Ultimately, however, the future of the Packer plans lay in the hands of the general public. If the cricket-watching public attended or watched the televised games in numbers sufficient to make it a financial proposition for its instigators, then the revolution would grow and eventually there would have to be compromise between established cricket and Mr Packer's organization. With public support, Packer knows he can go ahead with his wide-ranging plans for schoolboy coaching (already $200,000 had been earmarked for a junior coaching campaign in New South Wales) and even intervention at club and interstate level. If, as I suspect, public support is not great enough, the troupe could die within a year.

Whatever happens, cricket as it known has been terribly scarred. Hopefully the scars will heal in time and the many lessons learnt from them will be put into action to benefit the game. The one question remaining then is: is it 23.59 o'clock or 00.01? Is the game passing through midnight into the dawn of a new era of progress? Or is it entering a darkness of bitterness and division that will tear cricket apart?

APPENDIX

JUBILEE (FIRST) TEST

England v. Australia
at Lord's, 16, 17, 18, 20, 21 June 1977
Umpires: W. L. Budd, H. D. Bird
Toss won by M. Brearley (England)

ENGLAND

	First innings		Second Innings	
D. Amiss	b. Thomson	4	b. Thomson	0
M. Brearley	c. Robinson b. Thomson	9	c. Robinson b. O'Keeffe	49
R. Woolmer	run out	79	c. Chappell b. Pascoe	120
D. Randall	c. Chappell b. Walker	53	c. McCosker b. Thomson	0
A. Greig	b. Pascoe	5	c. O'Keeffe b. Pascoe	91
G. Barlow	c. McCosker b. Walker	1	lbw b. Pascoe	5
A. Knott	c. Walters b. Thomson	8	c. Walters b. Walker	8
C. Old	c. Marsh b. Walker	9	c. Walters b. Walker	0
J. Lever	b. Pascoe	8	c. Marsh b. Thomson	3
D. Underwood	not out	11	not out	12
R. Willis	b. Thomson	17	c. Marsh b. Thomson	0
Sundries		12		17
TOTAL	all out	216	all out	305

Fall of wicket: 12; 13; 111; 121; 134; 155; 171; 183; 189; 216.
0; 132; 224; 263; 286; 286; 286; 286; 305; 305.

Bowling (O-M-R-W) J. Thomson 20.5-5-41-4; L. Pascoe 23-7-53-2; M. Walker 30-6-66-3; K. O'Keeffe 10-3-32-0; G. Chappell 3-0-12-0.
J. Thomson 24.4-3-86-4; L. Pascoe 26-2-96-3; M. Walker 35-13-56-2; G. Chappell 12-2-24-0; K. O'Keeffe 15-7-26-1.

AUSTRALIA

	First innings		Second Innings	
R. Robinson	b. Lever	11	c. Woolmer b. Old	4
R. McCosker	b. Old	23	b. Willis	1
G. Chappell	c. Old b. Willis	66	c. Lever b. Old	24
C. Serjeant	c. Knott b. Willis	81	c. Amiss b. Underwood	3
D. Walters	c. Brearley b. Willis	53	c. sub (Ealham) b. Underwood	10
D. Hookes	c. Brearley b. Old	11	c. and b. Willis	50
R. Marsh	lbw b. Willis	1	not out	6
K. O'Keeffe	c. sub (Ealham) b. Willis	12	not out	8
M. Walker	c. Knott b. Willis	4		
J. Thomson	b. Willis	6		
L. Pascoe	not out	3		
Sundries		25		8
TOTAL	all out	296	for 6 wickets	114

Fall: 25; 51; 135; 238; 256; 264; 265; 284; 290; 296.
5; 48; 64; 71; 102.

R. Willis 10.1-40-2; C. Old 14 0 46 2; D. Under...

at Old Trafford, Manchester, 7, 8, 9, 11, 12 July 1977
Umpires: W. E. Alley, T. W. Spencer
Toss won by G. Chappell (Australia)

AUSTRALIA

	First innings		Second innings	
R. McCosker	c. Old b. Willis	2	c. Underwood b. Willis	0
I. Davis	c. Knott b. Old	34	c. Lever b. Willis	12
G. Chappell	c. Knott b. Greig	44	b. Underwood	112
C. Serjeant	lbw b. Lever	14	c. Woolmer b. Underwood	8
D. Walters	c. Greig b. Miller	88	lbw b. Greig	10
D. Hookes	c. Knott b. Lever	5	c. Brearley b. Miller	28
R. Marsh	c. Amiss b. Miller	36	c. Randall b. Underwood	1
R. Bright	c. Greig b. Lever	12	c. and b. Underwood	0
K. O'Keeffe	c. Knott b. Willis	12	not out	24
M. Walker	b. Underwood	9	c. Greig b. Underwood	6
J. Thomson	not out	14	c. Randall b. Underwood	1
Sundries		27		16
TOTAL	all out	297	all out	218

Fall of wicket: 4; 80; 96; 125; 140; 238; 246; 272; 272; 297.
0; 30; 74; 92; 146; 147; 147; 202; 212; 218.
Bowling (O-M-R-W) R. Willis 21-8-45-2; J. Lever 25-8-60-3; C. Old 20-3-57-1; D. Underwood 20.2-7-53-1; A. Greig 13-4-37-1; G. Miller 10-3-18-2. R. Willis 16-2-56-2; J. Lever 4-1-10-0; D. Underwood 32.5-13-66-6; C. Old 8-1-26-0; A. Greig 12-6-19-1; G. Miller 9-2-24-1.

ENGLAND

	First innings		Second innings	
D. Amiss	c. Chappell b. Walker	11	not out	28
M. Brearley	c. Chappell b. Thomson	6	c. Walters b. O'Keeffe	44
R. Woolmer	lbw b. O'Keeffe	137	not out	0
D. Randall	c. Davis b. Bright	79		
A. Greig	c. and b. Walker	76		
A. Knott	c. O'Keeffe b. Thomson	39		
G. Miller	c. Marsh b. Thomson	6		
C. Old	c. Marsh b. Walker	37		
J. Lever	b. Bright	10		
D. Underwood	b. Bright	10		
R. Willis	not out	1		
Sundries		25		10
TOTAL	all out	437	for 1 wicket	82

Fall: 19; 23; 165; 325; 348; 366; 377; 404; 435; 437.
75.
Bowling (O-M-R-W) J. Thomson 38-11-73-3; M. Walker 54-15-131-3; R. Bright 35.1-11-69-3; K. O'Keeffe 36-11-114-1; G. Chappell 6-1-25-0. J. Thomson 8-2-24-0; M. Walker 7-0-17-0; K. O'Keeffe 9.1-4-25-1; R. Bright 5-2-6-0.

ENGLAND WON BY 9 WICKETS

THIRD TEST

England v. Australia
at Trent Bridge, Nottingham, 28, 29, 30 July; 1, 2 August 1977
Umpires: H. D. Bird, D. J. Constant
Toss won by G. Chappell (Australia)

AUSTRALIA

Batsman	First innings		Second innings	
R. McCosker	c. Brearley b. Hendrick	51	c. Brearley b. Willis	107
I. Davis	c. Botham b. Underwood	33	c. Greig b. Willis	9
G. Chappell	b. Botham	19	b. Hendrick	27
D. Hookes	c. Hendrick b. Willis	17	lbw b. Hendrick	42
D. Walters	c. Hendrick b. Botham	11	c. Randall b. Greig	28
R. Robinson	c. Brearley b. Greig	11	lbw b. Underwood	34
R. Marsh	lbw b. Botham	0	c. Greig b. Willis	0
K. O'Keeffe	not out	48	not out	21
M. Walker	c. Hendrick b. Botham	0	b. Willis	17
J. Thomson	c. Knott b. Botham	21	b. Willis	0
L. Pascoe	c. Greig b. Hendrick	20	c. Hendrick b. Underwood	0
Sundries		12		24
TOTAL	all out	243	all out	309

Fall of wicket: 79; 101; 131; 133; 153; 153; 155; 196; 243.
18; 60; 154; 204; 240; 240; 270; 307; 308; 309.

Bowling (O-M-R-W) R. Willis 15-0-58-1; M. Hendrick 21.1-6-46-2;
I. Botham 20-5-74-5; A. Greig 15-4-35-1; D. Underwood 11-5-18-1.
R. Willis 26-4-88-5; M. Hendrick 32-14-56-2; I.
Botham 25-5-60-0; D. Underwood 27-15-49-2;
A. Greig 9-2-24-1; G. Miller 5-2-5-0;
R. Woolmer 3-0-3-0.

ENGLAND

Batsman	First innings		Second innings	
M. Brearley	c. Hookes b. Pascoe	15	b. Walker	81
G. Boycott	c. McCosker b. Thomson	107	not out	80
R. Woolmer	lbw b. Pascoe	0		
D. Randall	run out	13	not out	19
A. Greig	b. Thomson	11	b. Walker	0
G. Miller	c. Robinson b. Pascoe	13		
A. Knott	c. Davis b. Thomson	135	c. O'Keeffe b. Walker	2
I. Botham	c. Walker	25		
D. Underwood	b. Pascoe	7		
M. Hendrick	b. Walker	1		
R. Willis	not out	2		
Sundries		35		7
TOTAL	all out	364	for 3 wickets	189

Fall: 34; 34; 52; 64; 82; 297; 326; 357; 357; 364.
154; 156; 158.

Bowling (O-M-R-W) J. Thomson 31-6-103-3; L. Pascoe 32-10-80-4; J. Thomson 16-6-34-0; L. Pascoe 22-6-43-0;
M. Walker 39.2-12-79-2; G. Chappell 8-0-19-0; K. O'Keeffe 11-4-43-0; K. O'Keeffe 19.2-2-65-0; M. Walker 24-8-40-3.

England v. Australia
at Headingley, Leeds, 11, 12, 13, 15, 16 August 1977
Umpires: W. E. Alley, W. L. Budd
Toss won by M. Brearley (England)

ENGLAND

	First innings		Second innings	
M. Brearley	c. Marsh b. Thomson	0		
G. Boycott	c. Chappell b. Pascoe	191		
R. Woolmer	c. Chappell b. Thomson	37		
D. Randall	lbw b. Pascoe	20		
A. Greig	b. Thomson	43		
G. Roope	c. Walters b. Thomson	34		
A. Knott	lbw b. Bright	57		
I. Botham	b. Bright	0		
D. Underwood	c. Bright b. Pascoe	6		
M. Hendrick	c. Robinson b. Pascoe	4		
R. Willis	not out	5		
Sundries		39		
TOTAL	all out	436		

Fall of wicket: 0; 82; 105; 201; 275; 398; 398; 412; 422; 436.
Bowling (O-M-R-W) J. Thomson 34-7-113-4; M. Walker 48-21-97-0;
L. Pascoe 34.4-10-91-4; D. Walters 3-1-5-0.

AUSTRALIA

	First innings		Second innings	
R. McCosker	run out	27	c. Knott b. Greig	12
I. Davis	lbw b. Hendrick	0	c. Knott b. Greig	19
G. Chappell	c. Brearley b. Hendrick	4	c. Greig b. Willis	36
D. Hookes	lbw b. Botham	24	lbw b. Hendrick	21
D. Walters	c. Hendrick b. Botham	4	lbw b. Woolmer	15
R. Robinson	c. Greig b. Hendrick	20	b. Hendrick	20
R. Marsh	c. Knott b. Botham	2	c. Randall b. Hendrick	63
R. Bright	not out	9	c. Greig b. Hendrick	5
M. Walker	c. Knott b. Botham	7	b. Willis	30
J. Thomson	b. Botham	0	b. Willis	0
L. Pascoe	b. Hendrick	0	not out	0
Sundries		6		27
TOTAL	all out	103	all out	248

Fall: 8; 26; 52; 57; 66; 77; 87; 100; 100; 103.
Bowling (O-M-R-W) R. Willis 5-0-35-0; M. Hendrick 15.3-2-41-4; I.
Botham 11-3-21-5.
31; 35; 63; 97; 130; 167; 179; 244; 245; 248.
R. Willis 14-2-32-3; M. Hendrick 22.5-6-54-4;
A. Greig 20-7-64-2; I. Botham 17-3-47-0;
R. Woolmer 8-4-8-1; D. Underwood 8-3-16-0.

ENGLAND WON BY AN INNINGS AND 85 RUNS

FIFTH TEST

England v. Australia
at The Oval, 25, 26, 27, 29, 30 August 1977
Umpires: D. J. Constant, T. W. Spencer
Toss won by G. Chappell (Australia)

ENGLAND

	First innings		Second innings	
M. Brearley	c. Marsh b. Malone	39	c. Serjeant b. Thomson	4
G. Boycott	c. McCosker b. Walker	39	not out	25
R. Woolmer	lbw b. Thomson	15	c. Marsh b. Malone	6
D. Randall	c. Marsh b. Malone	3	not out	20
A. Greig	c. Bright b. Malone	0		
G. Roope	b. Thomson	38		
A. Knott	c. McCosker b. Malone	6		
J. Lever	lbw b. Malone	3		
D. Underwood	b. Thomson	20		
M. Hendrick	b. Thomson	15		
R. Willis	not out	24		
Sundries		12		2
TOTAL	all out	214	for 2 wickets	57

Fall of wicket: 86; 88; 104; 106; 121; 130; 169; 174; 214.
5; 16.
Bowling (O-M-R-W) J. Thomson 23.2-3-87-4; M. Malone 47-20-63-5;
J. Thomson 5-1-22-1; M. Malone 10-4-14-1; M.
M. Walker 28-11-51-1; R. Bright 3-2-1-0.
Walker 8-2-14-0; R. Bright 3-2-5-0.

AUSTRALIA

C. Serjeant	lbw b. Willis	0
R. McCosker	lbw b. Willis	32
G. Chappell	c. and b. Underwood	39
K. Hughes	c. Willis b. Hendrick	1
D. Hookes	c. Knott b. Greig	85
D. Walters	b. Willis	4
R. Marsh	lbw b. Hendrick	57
R. Bright	lbw b. Willis	16
M. Walker	not out	78
M. Malone	b. Lever	46
J. Thomson	b. Willis	17
Sundries		10
TOTAL	all out	385

Fall: 0; 54; 67; 84; 104; 184; 236; 252; 352; 385.
Bowling (O-M-R-W) R. Willis 29.3-5-102-5; M. Hendrick 37-5-93-2;

AVERAGES

ENGLAND
BATTING

	Matches	Innings	N.O.	Runs	HS	Ave
G. Boycott	3	5	2	442	191	147.33
R. A. Woolmer	5	8	1	394	137	56.28
A. P. E. Knott	5	7	0	255	135	36.42
G. R. J. Roope	2	2	0	72	38	36.00
D. W. Randall	5	8	2	207	79	34.50
A. W. Greig	5	7	0	226	91	32.28
J. M. Brearley	5	9	0	247	81	27.44
R. G. D. Willis	5	6	4	49	24*	24.50
D. L. Underwood	5	6	2	66	20	16.50
C. M. Old	2	3	0	46	37	15.33
D. L. Amiss	2	4	1	43	28*	14.33
I. T. Botham	2	2	0	25	25	12.50
G. Miller	2	2	0	19	13	9.50
M. Hendrick	3	3	0	20	15	6.66
J. K. Lever	3	4	0	24	10	6.00

Played in one Test: G. D. Barlow 1, 5.*
* Not out

BOWLING

	Overs	Maidens	Runs	Wickets	Ave
R. G. D. Willis	166.4	36	534	27	19.77
I. T. Botham	73	16	202	10	20.20
M. Hendrick	128.4	33	290	14	20.71
D. L. Underwood	169.1	61	362	13	27.84
A. W. Greig	77	25	196	7	28.00
J. K. Lever	75	22	197	5	39.40
C. M. Old	77	14	199	5	39.80

Also bowled: G. Miller 24-7-47-3; R. A. Woolmer 16-5-31-1.

AUSTRALIA
BATTING

	Matches	Innings	N.O.	Runs	HS	Ave
K. J. O'Keeffe	3	6	4	125	48*	62.50
G. S. Chappell	5	9	0	371	112	41.22
D. W. Hookes	5	9	0	283	85	31.44
R. B. McCosker	5	9	0	255	107	28.33
K. D. Walters	5	9	0	223	88	24.77
M. H. N. Walker	5	8	1	151	78*	21.57
C. S. Serjeant	3	5	0	106	81	21.20
R. W. Marsh	5	9	1	166	63	20.75
I. C. Davis	3	6	0	107	34	17.83
R. D. Robinson	3	6	0	100	34	16.66
R. J. Bright	3	5	1	42	16	10.50
J. R. Thomson	5	8	1	59	21	8.42
L. S. Pascoe	3	5	2	23	20	7.66

Played in one Test: K. J. Hughes 1; M. F. Malone 46.

BOWLING

	Overs	Maidens	Runs	Wickets	Ave
M. F. Malone	57	24	77	6	12.83
J. R. Thomson	200.2	44	583	23	25.34
L. S. Pascoe	137.4	35	363	13	27.92
R. J. Bright	72.1	27	147	5	29.40
M. H. N. Walker	273.2	78	551	14	39.35

Also bowled: G. S. Chappell 39-5-105-0; K. J. O'Keeffe 100.3-31-305-3; K. D. Walters 6-1-10-0.